Auras

See Them in Only 60 Seconds!

Mark Smith

Foreword by
Raymond A. Moody, M.D., Ph.D.

2000
Llewellyn Publications
St. Paul, Minnesota 55164-0383

FIRST EDITION
Fifth printing, 2000

Author photo by William R. Reckert
Cover design by Anne Marie Garrison
Cover photograph by Dana Wheelock Photography
Editing and book design by Rebecca Zins
Interior illustration by Wendy Frogge´t

Previously published as *In a New Light* (Aurora Publishing, Bethesda, MD) © 1996 by Mark T. Smith.

Library of Congress Cataloging-in-Publication Data
Smith, Mark, 1953-
    Auras: see them in only 60 seconds! / Mark Smith; foreword by Raymond Moody.—1st ed.
        p.   cm.
    ISBN 1-56718-643-2 (trade paper)
    1. Aura   I. Title
BF1389.A8S55 1997   97-9984
133.8'92—dc21   CIP

Llewellyn Worldwide does not participate in, endorse, or have any authority or responsibility concerning private business transactions between our authors and the public.
    All mail addressed to the author is forwarded but the publisher cannot, unless specifically instructed by the author, give out an address or phone number.

Llewellyn Publications
A Division of Llewellyn Worldwide, Ltd.
P.O. Box 64383
St. Paul, MN 55164-0383
www.llewellyn.com

Printed in the United States of America

Seeing Is Believing!

Auras: See Them in Only 60 Seconds! is a personal exploration of the vital role auric perception can play in your life as a method for maintaining health and well-being. Seeing the human aura is perfectly natural and safe. Many people are already aware of auras, but tend to think of them in terms of getting a vibe or feeling chemistry.

Once you've mastered the skill of seeing auras, you will be able to tell when someone is lying, what their profession is, and detect illnesses before they manifest physically. Learn how to promote healing by meditating upon particular colors. Seeing the aura is the first step into a bigger world of increased awareness and alternative healing modalities such as bioenergy therapy.

Mark Smith has appeared around the country on college campuses and TV and radio talk shows demonstrating his simple and effective techniques. Now you can see auras for yourself by following the easy ten-step program in this book. Isn't it time you saw what everyone is talking about?

About the Author

Toward the end of his life, my father wrote that I was "perhaps the most creative and happy person [he had] ever known." My fellow Jesuit brothers likened my persona to a "perpetual kid at Christmas." All I know is that I was fortunate enough to pick great parents, grow up in an extremely stimulating environment, and somehow manage to avoid self-destruction while running pell-mell through life as if it were my own personal all-you-can-eat buffet.

So, you might say my whole life's experiences are my credentials, which allow me to write from a curious student-participant viewpoint. The transformations that have occurred for me in this process of uncovering and (finally) understanding what I do know to be true are my driving motives for writing. I want to spread the good news and let everybody in on the secrets.

How to Write to the Author

If you wish to contact the author or would like more information about this book, please write to the author in care of Llewellyn Worldwide, and we will forward your request. We cannot guarantee that every letter written to the author can be answered, but all will be forwarded. Please write to:

Mark Smith
% Llewellyn Worldwide
P.O. Box 64383, Dept. K643-2
St. Paul, MN 55164-0383, U.S.A.

Please enclose a self-addressed, stamped envelope for reply, or $1.00 to cover costs. If outside U.S.A., enclose international postal reply coupon.

Or e-mail the author at:

aurorasmit@aol.com

Also look for the Internet home page at:

http://www.aurorasmith.com/aura

For my father,

William Anthony Smith.

Requiem aeternam dona ei Domine,
et lux perpetua leceat ei.

Grant him eternal rest O Lord,
and let perpetual light shine upon him.

Contents

Acknowledgments

I would like to recognize the following people for their love and help over the years, making my life (and this book) possible.

John Fatland, M.D.
Russell Tilley, M.D.
Raymond Moody, M.D., Ph.D.
Rev. C. John McCloskey III
Rev. Francis Burch, S.J.
Robert Montague
Robert McEachern
Chalmers Wood II
Constance Abbott
Mary Phillips
Patricia Heller

Foreword

We're all really lucky, it seems to me, to be living in an era in which we have given ourselves permission to reexplore the old spiritual modalities that for so long have been relegated to the dusty back rooms of the mind. What in the world is an aura? How many times over the last twenty years have I been approached by someone who excitedly and cheerfully praises me for the vibrant color and wise deportment of my aura? And I, for my part, always proudly accept the compliment, even though I've never had any idea what they were talking about.

Until now.

Hallelujah! I am pleased that my wonderful friend Mark Smith has put down a great deal of information on this hazy subject. I am especially pleased that he has made his new book into a manual—actual exercises to perform—so that I can finally see for myself.

Mark writes here not from the perspective of some abstractly esoterical theoretical construct, but from his own personal experiences that he has had as he waded out into this most peculiar dimension of the human mind and spirit. And as I know him as a friend, and as a fine and sensitive person, I look forward to retracing his steps through this intriguing new labyrinth.

For the uninformed on this subject, such as myself, his work—free as it is of incomprehensible verbiage—seems the ideal place to begin. And I suspect that many others will be probing this realm, too, with this guidebook in their hands.

Raymond A. Moody, M.D., Ph.D.

Preface

Having grown up in the Kenwood area near Washington, D.C., on a cherry tree–lined street that rained pink and white blossoms in the springtime, I was accustomed at a young age to natural beauty and a wonderfully loving, fully functional family. My Montessori schoolteacher mother, who stayed at home until I finished grade school, encouraged me to be anything I wanted to be. Taking an early interest in both music and science (wanting a violin for my third birthday and a chemistry set the following Christmas), my curiosity was broadly based—but cruelly taxing on her nerves! This, coupled with a propensity for knives inserted into light and electrical sockets and a love for all things pyrotechnic, made my minding a full-time job. When I wasn't climbing the bookcase (and pulling it down on top of me), I was releasing the parking brakes of cars parked in the neighbors' driveways. I thought nothing of walking into their houses unannounced and turning on their hi-fi's or playing their pianos. No wonder they had a block party the day I started school, making me shake their hands, congratulating me on surviving to the ripe old age of five!

Survival up to that point, however, was by no means assured, nor were the risks limited to self-destructive tendencies or neighbors who wanted to kill me. In fact, I almost "checked out" at birth, being six weeks premature and under three pounds in weight. Because I was thought to be hydrocephalic, the doctor didn't give me much chance for survival, especially since the thermostat in the incubator at the Sangley Point Navy Base near Cavite City in the Philippines was broken and kept trying to fry me. My navy commander father had some clout, and within forty-eight hours was able to arrange for a seaplane to fly Dr. John Fatland (U.S.N.), with me in his arms, up north to Clark Air Force Base—and to a properly functioning incubator. Told I probably wouldn't survive the trip, my devoutly religious parents credit divine intervention (and the U.S. Navy) with my safety and survival.

It was at this time that I had my first out-of-body experience and my only near-death experience—as vivid today as it was when it happened. I found myself floating above my isolet, looking down at this red, prunelike form with tubes attached, and wondering if there wasn't some mistake. This couldn't be the body I was supposed to be in. Something was wrong here, and I didn't like it.

As I hovered near the ceiling of this room shaped like an L, I was aware of both hot and cold sensations, with heat coming from directly above and cold emanating lower. I also remember the walls being a purple color. My isolet was off in the short end of the L, separate from the other babies down in the long end of the room. Then a voice that spoke telepathically said I should go back into that body and that everything would be fine, not to worry. For one of the few times in my life, I was instantly obedient.

Whenever asked what my first memory was, even as a child of three or four years of age, I referred to this experience. I also remember, from about that time, vivid images of guardian angels, sometimes as many as seven, more often two or three at a time. Also quite vivid is the memory of telling my mother that "when we die, it's like waking up from a life of dreams." She would look at me with a puzzled but supportive expression and say "ah . . . that's right, dear."

It wasn't until the fifth grade—at 11:30 A.M. on a Thursday morning during a math test on fractions—that I had my next out-of-body experience. Once again I was above my body, floating at the top of the ceiling, looking down on my head. And again the entire room was visible in a way that cannot be adequately described, but was instantly recognizable as similar to the near-death experience I had as a forty-eight-hour-old infant.

This spontaneous out-of-body experience was not caused by any type of trauma; I had a total of six by the time I was twenty-one, each more intense than the previous one. The cumulative effect of these experiences led me to believe I had a vocation in the priesthood. Never having heard of out-of-body experiences, cosmic consciousness, or astral projection, I had only the religious culture I was familiar with to try to make sense of these other states of consciousness. I also refer to them as "spiritual orgasms," for lack of a better description, since words are inadequate to fully cover the range of sensations and emotions these experiences evoke. But you *know* when you have one.

After college and a stint as a Jesuit candidate, my life took a new turn when I began touring the country as a professional musician, playing acoustic guitar and singing my own compositions, opening for groups like Jefferson Starship, Jeff Beck, and Grateful Dead members Bob Weir and Jerry Garcia's bands. I'd come a long way since my first piano recital at age four, playing now to 20,000 instead of 20.

I was also lecturing at college campuses across the country on handwriting analysis, doing TV appearances, and teaching people how to see auras.

But it was during a performance in Iowa that my life truly came full circle when I met the navy doctor who had delivered me thirty years before in the L-shaped, purple-walled room. John Fatland and his wife, Donita, had kept in touch with my parents over the years by religiously exchanging Christmas cards since our return from the Philippines. My mother alerted them to my concert schedule, which included a stop in Des Moines. My father need not have threatened to disown me should I fail to see them while I was there, because I was actually quite excited at the prospect of finally meeting my "birthing" parents.

Having never talked to or even seen a picture of them, I was somewhat apprehensive as I pulled in to the long driveway and approached the large colonial home surrounded by acres of rich farmland. But I was overcome with emotion as they came bounding out the front door and down the steps, arms outstretched to enfold me in a welcoming embrace. We all started crying many joyful tears, standing together, arms wrapped around each other, hugging and kissing.

This amazing moment was eclipsed only by revelations that yes, it had been an L-shaped room, and the walls had been painted mauve with paint left over from the redecoration of the admiral's quarters. They told me no one was supposed to know about the paint, since it was not navy regulation battleship gray; they had used it just to liven up the place. I was also told that I was put in the corner of the room, near the closet, to keep me away from the other infants, who might pass on germs.

I found out that Donita had been pregnant with fraternal twins when I was born, and that she had also delivered prematurely, losing the boy. They always felt a special kinship with me, thinking that I was "the one they saved." Dr. Fatland grew serious as he said, "I've done some research on this and can't find a smaller surviving baby on record the year you were born. I don't know why you're here, but you're definitely here for a reason."

So too, I think, are we all.

1

Seeing the Aura

*This was the start of a journey
that never ends. As I learned more,
I learned how little I knew.*

It couldn't possibly happen. There is no way you can see an aura! Maybe in your dreams, or in old paintings of the saints, but not here, not now, not in my living room!

But that's exactly what I was seeing almost twenty years ago as my friend was standing right in front of me explaining the simple techniques anybody can learn. Even, apparently, skeptics like me. Maybe I didn't see colors, and the shape and intensity was constantly changing, but there was no doubt about it. That bright silvery envelope was one to three inches around his head and shoulders, and it wasn't going away. In fact, the more I looked, the brighter and larger it became!

That's how it all started. That's how I got hooked. Within a few days, I could see colors. Then I found out I could see my own aura in the mirror using the same basic technique. I started reading books—mostly esoteric, out-of-print guides on color meditation—explaining what each color meant and what part of the body each color's vibration affected. It was as if a door to a wholly new world had opened up to me. This was a world that was going on all around me, a world the ancients and wise people from every age knew and took for granted.

This was the start of a journey that never ends. As I learned more, I learned how little I knew. And it all started that late summer afternoon as the sun cast a soft, even light in my old studio apartment three floors above N Street just outside Georgetown.

How to View the Aura

Here's how you, too, can "see the light":

Stand the subject eighteen inches in front of a plain white background. Have the person relax and breathe deeply. For best viewing, you need to be at least ten feet away, and the lights should not be too bright or focused directly on the subject. Natural lighting is best. The technique to view the aura requires that you look *past* the head and shoulder area. Focus on the wall behind the figure. As you stare past the outline of the body, you will very quickly notice a fuzzy white or grayish silver envelope surrounding the body. It almost looks like a light is behind the person, pointing up.

Then most probably it will disappear.

That is because the natural reaction of most people as they first see this envelope is to inadvertently change their focus to the person and not continue to stare at the wall. As soon as you go back to focusing on the background, the envelope will reappear. You must train your eye not to revert to normal focus—that is the hardest thing to learn. Once you have mastered maintaining your gaze through the person, you will notice that colors, shapes, rays, and even secondary auric fields will be readily visible.

Seeing beyond the Envelope

It may take some time. Although I could see the envelope, or as some say, "Casper the friendly ghost," right away, it was three days before I saw colors—but what colors! Yellow or pink is first for most people, then blue, green, or purple. Some of you lucky ones will see color right away.

A few people I have trained never see any color, with the exception of yellow now and then, but everyone has at least seen the envelope. If you wear glasses, taking them off might help, although some students do better keeping them on. The type of light is also a controlling factor. Fluorescent light is the worst; natural indirect light is the best. Direct sunlight is too strong and will overpower and wash out the aura. Candlelight is very good, but be careful the candle does not cast shadows on the viewing background.

Try various subjects. Get them to breathe deeply and exhale fully. One hint: Have them recite the alphabet slowly, taking breaths after every two letters. Then speed up after the letter M, finishing all the rest of the letters without taking a breath, if possible.

You'll see a change in the aura as the breathing pattern changes. On some people, as they speed up, the aura will expand. If they are not breathing correctly, that is, shallowly, it will actually shrink. Breathing fully and deeply is the single most energizing exercise you can do. When the subject inhales, the aura should appear to shrink slightly, and when the subject exhales fully, it will appear to expand. If the subject's breathing pattern changes to shallow breathing, the aura may appear very weak and close to the body.

Another helpful hint: Have the subject rock gently from side to side. You will see the aura move with the person. Sometimes it stays right with the subject, while with others it will lag behind. You might see a ball of color over one shoulder, or a strong, bright line of light down one arm. These may pulsate and then vanish.

Color Vibrations

There is no right or wrong aura, no one color better than another. Some shades of colors may indicate less desirable aspects, but the brightness and clarity of the aura denotes various stages of wellness, peace, and happiness. Clear and bright is better than dull and murky. The charts at the end of the book will illuminate the color spectrum and should be taken as a general guide to understanding each color's meaning.

Most often, auras have a base color that is close to the body and radiates no more than one to three inches from the head and shoulder area (although the body is surrounded by the aura, it is easiest to see around the head and shoulder area). This color may be mixed with another color, usually the next higher or lower color on the spectrum of light.

For example, a yellow base will mix with green or orange and might appear chartreuse one moment, revert to yellow as you continue to stare, and then turn once more to orangish pink before stabilizing around yellow.

The human aura is generally not stable, changing according to internal as well as external stimuli. Everything we do, say, or think influences our energy field. The color we radiate is affected by our physical surroundings as well as by the people we come in contact with and the energy fields they radiate. What we eat and drink, and any medication we take, contributes to our overall picture. Even our breathing patterns change the aura, as you saw in the previous exercise.

We all talk about "vibes" or "chemistry" between people. First impressions are formed in an instant. Much of this is due to visual clues: general attractiveness, facial expression, clothing, physical presence, and posture. Positively or negatively, we consciously analyze and rate other individuals within seconds after we meet. Subconsciously we do the same thing: vibes, or chemistry, may be intangible, but the interaction of energy fields provides us with gut instincts that may be more subtle, but just as telling, about the ultimate level of compatibility.

This is why you won't like some people whom others may be drawn to or why you'll like someone immediately who might not be the most physically attractive. They just have a certain something you can't put your finger on that attracts or repels you. This something just might be our electromagnetic vibration, which is visible to us as the aura when light passes through it (and felt when we become sensitive through training in bioenergy therapy).

The speed of the vibration determines what color we see. Red, which is at the base of the color spectrum, is a long, slow wave. Orange, yellow, and green are progressively shorter, faster waves, and easier to see. Blue and violet are the fastest and hardest to see, typically showing up in the outer (astral) aura, which is distinct from the brighter inner (etheric) aura we first learn to see. Some people do possess violet in their inner aura, and it denotes great spiritual attainment. Seen in the outer aura, it shows great spiritual capability. Likewise, gold is a highly evolved color and shows great power. It might appear as a ball of energy above the head or on top of one shoulder.

In classes I've taught, students have actually seen golden rays radiating upward from some subjects, or geometric shapes, like triangles, around others. Some subjects appear to be wearing dunce caps that extend two to three feet above their heads. These phenomena are witnessed by up to sixty people at a time, and when asked to write down descriptions of what they saw, a majority would corroborate these images in great detail.

Working Out Your View

So, now you have the basic technique to see the aura! Like any other muscle, you need to "work out" to develop and maintain the strength of this newfound ability. Try several different people in several different surroundings, keeping in mind the basics: white or neutral-colored wall, indirect lighting, and the subject at least eighteen inches away from the wall and ten feet from you. Most importantly, stay focused on the wall, not on your subject.

Now, isn't finding one of your long-lost sixth senses fun? You can even see your own aura in the mirror. Just throw your focus on the wall or whatever is behind your image, and as you stare (and breathe), you'll see it.

Don't be discouraged if you don't see colors right away. Relax and keep trying. When you do see colors, you might gasp or make some kind of exclamation,

Auras

because the colors, although subtle at first, are actually quite intense. With practice, you can begin to see auras in a variety of settings, under various lighting conditions, and in front of less-than-optimum backgrounds. With any luck, this newfound talent will become second nature.

2

The Auric Touch

*Could it be that before we became
saturated with all the modern forms
of media, we were routinely able to
see auras? Is it possible that these abilities
are suppressed by our reliance on technology
and our faith in science?*

In pictures you have seen of angels or holy men and women, they invariably are depicted with light surrounding their heads or sometimes their whole bodies. Often rays of light are shown emanating from behind the head and shoulders in a geometric fashion. This is true in all cultures and religions. Buddha, Mohammed, Vishnu, Moses, the prophets, the saints, and Jesus Christ are all shown to be enveloped in light, usually golden, silver, or clear in color.

9

Could it be that before we became saturated with all the modern forms of media, we were routinely able to see auras? Is it possible that these abilities are suppressed by our reliance on technology and our faith in science? Have we let the conscious, rational mind totally discount our subconscious selves? Perhaps a rediscovery of these innate talents will open up a whole new (old) world and provide enrichment not found in modern forms of entertainment.

Certainly, my life has been changed with the discovery and use of these skills: first seeing the aura, then feeling it. In fact, my life was probably saved by the use of bioenergy and the therapeutic techniques involved in healing through the auric field. This actually happened on my first visit to the house of Mietek (pronounced *me' a-tek*) Wirkus, an émigré from what was then Communist Poland. It was 1986. Mietek, his wife, and his daughter had recently come to the United States and were starting to introduce bioenergy techniques in the Washington, D.C., area. They brought with them a wealth of knowledge and experience new to the West but used extensively throughout the eastern bloc and the Soviet Union.

Mietek had demonstrated unusual healing gifts as a child. The Kirlian Institute in Leningrad and the Popov Institute in Moscow were working on bioenergy phenomena in the early 1970s. Mietek trained himself in these healing techniques and later worked for various medical centers in Poland, such as the Isis Medical Clinic in Warsaw, and sometimes saw more than 100 patients a day. As incredible as it seems, he was able to help these people without becoming physically exhausted himself. He learned the secret of this tremendous endurance through studies with a Tibetan teacher, who taught him the "breath of youth." Once learned, it allows a person to let great amounts of energy channel through the body without causing fatigue or burnout. Remember how changing the breathing pattern changed the aura you saw? The effect of proper breathing cannot be overemphasized for maintaining good health: it is one of the most important factors in the transference of energy.

These bioenergy therapy sessions are conducted as a faster (and frequently better) way to treat illnesses such as fever, cramps, muscle spasms, and neuralgic disorders, allowing the surgical physicians to function more effectively in a critical-care role. Used in conjunction with standard Western medicine, bioenergy therapy was found by the doctors in Poland and the Soviet Union—who incorporated these techniques starting in the early 1980s—to be most beneficial in pre- and postoperative cases, reducing pain and promoting quicker recovery without the side effects associated with drugs.

When I first met Mietek, I was teaching a class on auras at the Burmese Embassy in Washington, D.C. Each month, about sixty people came to learn the simple technique described in Chapter 1. It was in this ideal surrounding of a large alabaster ballroom with crystal chandeliers and mirrors that the techniques for seeing the aura were mastered.

At this time a student came to me with an article about a man who not only saw auras but healed people without ever touching them. The following month, I was surprised to find this man, Mietek, and his family in my class. He spoke no English but could understand much of what was said; his multilingual wife, Margaret, filled in the rest. She told me how happy they were that someone in America was doing this work, and they seemed genuinely impressed with the content and form of the lecture I had just given.

Margaret asked me if I might like to come to their house for dinner, where we would discuss the possibility of my teaching visual auric techniques to their bio-energy students.

Curiosity was a main factor in my acceptance of their invitation, but I also felt a sense of fate drawing me toward them and their new and strange world—it is as if I knew that I was being called to do something I would have never chosen to do on my own. My natural skepticism was going into overdrive, and I certainly didn't have a belief structure based in the occult. But then I would never have believed you could see an aura until it was casually pointed out to me. After all, my middle name really is Thomas.

3

Hands-on Encounter

I could feel his energy and warmth
immediately when he first put his hands
near my body—massaging and smoothing
my aura, drawing me upward. I was woozy
for some time after that. Very relaxed, but not
depleted. In fact, strangely elated, tingly. . . .

It may be difficult to believe that a person who was already teaching a class on how to see auras would be skeptical of bioenergy therapy, but I was highly dubious, with a definite "show me" attitude. This skepticism remained throughout my first meeting with Mietek, when this course of study was described to me in detail, but I agreed to teach his students whenever needed. At the end of the evening, almost as a lark, I asked Mietek if he would "do" me.

Not knowing anything about the technique, I determined that I would be an objective observer and vowed not to give in to whatever lay ahead. I was strong and healthy, even though I was a little sore from overexertion at the previous day's softball game.

As he gently motioned for me to stand and step out to the center of the room, I made a silent check of all my body parts and found a sore right elbow from throwing the softball too hard, a sore left knee from sliding into second base in shorts, and a sore right tonsil. I was rather smug in my confidence that none of these minor ailments would be noticed. I would merely observe the technique, say something nice about how good it felt, thank them for dinner, and go home.

But a strange thing happened.

Not only did Mietek stop suddenly and work on each place that hurt, but he also found an area in my lower abdomen that he returned to twice, a place where I felt no pain. He also seemed to spend a lot of time in my heart area.

I could feel his energy and warmth immediately when he first put his hands around my aura—massaging and smoothing it, drawing me upward. I was woozy for some time after that. A lot like being tipsy, or just out of a sauna . . . very tingly. I wasn't sure what had happened, but I felt something, and that couldn't be denied. The feeling of warmth, especially when he lingered over a certain spot, was unmistakable. So was the light-headedness and feeling of calm relaxation.

I could definitely feel the energy, but my skepticism remained. Yes, he had discovered my sore spots, but he seemed much more concerned with my heart and stomach, which didn't hurt. After all, what could be wrong with them if I didn't have any pain in either region? It wasn't until one month later, when a sigmoidoscopic exam done after a routine checkup revealed a polyp in my colon, that my last vestige of skepticism vanished.

Reading Dis-Ease

How to explain the rest of the experience? I really needed to sit down for a moment after he finished, and I had this wonderful peaceful feeling. He was accurate about the knee, elbow, and tonsil, but more importantly, he was genuinely concerned about my heart. Margaret asked if I'd had a death in the family recently, or if I was under a lot of stress. "This could be causing a congestion of energy around your heart," she said, adding, "Do you drink?"

"A little," I said, remembering we drank wine at dinner.

"Good," she said. "A little red wine—or better yet, cognac—can be very good for your heart." I was wondering at this point how much *they* drank.

Actually, they seemed very sober, but I had many more questions now than answers and was ready to explore this phenomenon further. The knowledge that I would soon be meeting with their students made me even more curious. Maybe they would be able to prove or disprove the validity of what I had just experienced.

Margaret went on to say that some people experience cold or even sharp, brief flashes of pain when the energy touches an area of "dis-ease." At least I felt warmth and had been comfortable throughout the session, which lasted only about five minutes. Maybe he just read me wrong.

Then another strange thing happened.

Within a week, I noticed some blood in my stool. I contacted my family doctor, who recommended I get a full upper and lower gastrointestinal series along with a rectal exam. It was also necessary to look at my blood.

"You've got to take the blood test again. The lab must have screwed up," said the doctor. "There is no way your cholesterol and triglycerides could be so high." Normal readings are under 200 and 100, respectively; mine were 280 and 660! On the second try, cholesterol was down to 250, still considered somewhat worrisome, but triglycerides were up to 780.

"You have liquid fat for blood," the doctor told me in his best bedside manner. "The sample is coagulating in the test tube. It's amazing you haven't had coronary failure. Perhaps your quite normal blood pressure was the saving factor, along with the fact you don't smoke."

No wonder Mietek was concerned with my heart!

And then they found the polyp.

During the sigmoidoscopic exam, they discovered a one-centimeter growth, which turned out to be benign, inside my large intestine. "It could have been there since birth," my M.D. reassured me after it was removed. "It might have taken years to develop into cancer. In any case, it's gone now."

Once again, I was reminded of that first visit to the Wirkuses' house. They had warned me to get a checkup for my heart and stomach little more than a month before, and now I had just been through surgery and placed on a radical fat-free diet! My interest—and belief—in feeling the aura was definitely peaked.

4

The Teacher Goes to School

*What started out as curiosity soon
became profound excitement with each
new discovery of these hidden powers
within the human organism:
we could both send and receive energy!*

When I began teaching people how to see auras in
Mietek's classes, I found I was the only one there who was
not a health care professional. Physicians, nurses, chiro-
practic, osteopathic, and massage therapists of all denomi-
nations, and members of the psychiatric profession were
booking his classes months in advance. The reaction of
these mostly American Medical Association (AMA)–style
medical professionals was striking in that they seemed to

have come about their understanding of these alternate techniques cautiously, over time, but like myself had overcome their ingrained skepticism through personal experiences and the hard evidence that something was definitely happening.

What started out as curiosity, or in some cases a desire to debunk the notion that a person's health could be affected by massaging the aura, soon became profound excitement with each new discovery of these hidden powers within the human organism: we could both send and receive energy!

Finding My X-Energy

But what exactly is this energy that is apparently transferred from one individual to another? Paranormal expert John White has compiled more than 100 terms from ancient to modern sources for what he calls the "X-energy."

According to physics, there are four known forces of energy: electromagnetism, gravity, and the weak and strong nuclear forces. This X-energy, although currently unknown to physics, seems to be responsible for psychic or paranormal phenomena such as bioenergy transfer and the human aura. Research organizations such as the Institute for Noetic Sciences, the International Society for the Study of Energies, the International Society for the Study of Subtle Energy, and the International Association for New Science are all studying this scientific mystery.

Meanwhile, Mietek asked whether I wanted to study with him. After teaching three of his study groups, I'd become fascinated with the whole phenomenon, and it was at this point that he admitted me, his first non-medical professional. The classes were taught through his wife, Margaret, since Mietek spoke very little English at that point. He started each class (limited to twelve students) by scanning each student as we stood in a circle and held hands. The first thing I noticed was his very noisy and deep breathing: the so-called breath of youth. The second was the incredible warmth and tingling through the body as he placed his hands around my head and shoulders and in front of my chest and stomach, drawing the energy up my spine.

At first, the classes seemed too simple: relearning how to breathe, staring at a candle flame, visualizing a cave or safe haven, focusing on an orange dot on the wall. Each exercise was practiced for an entire month before we proceeded to the next one. As we progressed, we learned to incorporate each exercise with the one preceding it. Breathe, visualize, meditate; that's all we had to do.

Then we paired off and stared at each other's forehead, or third eye, chakra. We also stared into a mirror at our own third eye. Shapes changed, faces distorted, animals or old people appeared. It was quite disconcerting at first, but having a partner to share in the ordeal helped a lot. The face can even vanish if you stare long enough. We learned how to keep our eyes open for several minutes at a time, never once blinking. I wear contact lenses and can still go over ten minutes without blinking. During that time, the face I stared at—all the while staring just at the forehead—took on a kaleidoscopic panorama of people both younger and older, foreign, or even alien.

Then we learned how to feel the ball of energy between our hands. Soon after that, we felt the energy field of our partner. We put together all these techniques and exercises, and . . . it worked! We could feel as well as see the auric field and could raise this energy any time we wanted to. Experiments with physical objects in or near the auric field showed us how quickly and profoundly things such as magnets and crystals alter the natural state—and not always for the better.

Other elements, such as bee glue extract and amber, actually increase the auric field in color and intensity. These effects can be seen and felt. Suddenly we were no longer skeptical of these energy fields, but wondering when the medical establishment would start to incorporate these techniques. The amazing thing was that we had physicians in the class, and they were also saying these things!

In all, the basic classes took six months to complete. We continued to work on breathing and visualization techniques to increase our energy flow. It was almost shocking that at the end of these basic classes, we could see such changes in size and intensity of the aura and feel this ball of energy growing all around us. A few may have increased in some ways more than others, but we were all quite a bit more energetic than when we started.

5

A Most Interesting Event

*I was amazed by the incredible
accuracy of diagnoses, specifically the cranial
vertebra C-6 neck injury and the left
ovary problem, and all of this done on a
patient Mietek had never seen!*

Mietek told me I have a big third eye and would be a good candidate to learn advanced healing techniques. For those students who are selected and wish to continue, the advanced class delves into much greater detail about specific diseases and their treatment. These classes meet once a month and are much more anatomically oriented. We learn all the internal organs and the various parts of the brain. It reminded me a lot of biology classes I took in college. Fortunately, I already knew most of my physiognomy, but this was a good refresher course. We were given charts and diagrams of the body and taught how to scan the body, head to toe. Mietek, through Margaret, explained about meridians (a concept from the Chinese system of acupuncture) and energy flow to and from the chakras (energy centers in the body, according to yoga). He still started each class with the circle of students holding hands as he walked inside, smoothing our energy fields. During this period of study, we were asked to work with friends and relatives to gain practice and to experience new and different energy fields. We then met and discussed our experiences.

At the start of one class, after we broke the circle and sat down, he asked if we had run into any interesting cases. I raised my hand and described a therapy session that had occurred the previous day involving a woman complaining of migraines. Normally, by this time in my training, I could always feel some energy around the head of everyone I worked with. In this woman's case, even after some basic massage around the neck and shoulders, I could feel nothing. Finally, after twenty minutes of energy work, I could feel a slight cold tingle, but no warmth. She informed me that her migraines were fairly frequent in recent years and that sometimes they lasted for three or four days before subsiding. This one was severe and was in its third day, and I was a last resort, since medicine didn't seem to help. She left claiming some relief, but I knew I hadn't been very effective.

My question to Mietek was, "Do all migraine sufferers have total energy block above the neck?" Mietek became unusually animated and spoke to Margaret very rapidly in Polish. "Mark, how well do you know this girl? Are you romantically involved?" I worked with her in the office, and we'd been in a local theatrical production together (as the romantic leads in *Foxfire*), but we were not personally involved at all.

"Do you know her well enough to ask her some personal questions?"

I was a little puzzled when Margaret asked about what had occurred six years before: A car accident? Or a fall? Neck injuries to cranial vertebra C-5, C-6? Then she asked me to find out if my friend had problems with her left ovary. Did she have irregular menstrual cycles, and did the migraines fit into a sixty-day cycle of occurrence?

When I saw this woman next, she felt better, and I was able to ask her about her medical history, specifically about neck injuries, car accidents, irregular menstrual cycles, left ovary problems, and frequency and pattern of migraine attacks. As she proceeded to answer these questions, I could almost see the gears turning and the light bulb go on over her head. Yes, she did have a car accident six years ago, and cranial vertebra C-6 was damaged, which caused her first migraine. But the migraines went away until three years ago, when her left ovary was removed, and yes, the migraines started happening about every two months after that! She was excited to discover this link in her pattern of illness and was surprised she hadn't noticed the parallel between menstrual cycles and migraines before.

I was amazed by the incredible accuracy of diagnoses, specifically, the cranial vertebra C-6 neck injury and the left ovary problem—and all of this done on a patient Mietek had never seen!

I had to wait another month before I could ask Mietek my next question: "Is this the standard diagnosis for a woman with migraines?" Once again, Mietek spoke rapidly in Polish, and Margaret translated. "Mietek warned you not to take on the energy of the person you are helping. You must learn to block the energy from coming into you at your wrist. You Americans are so open and empathic, Mietek was able to read her illness from you even though you had seen her the day before. In your extra efforts to help her, you left yourself open and did not exercise your meditation and visualization techniques for your own protection."

I'm afraid I don't remember too much from the rest of that class. I was so overwhelmed by this demonstration that all I could say at the end of it was, "Twenty years from now, I'll be able to tell people I studied with the great Mietek Wirkus." Margaret laughed and in her typical humble generosity said, "Twenty years from now, people will say they worked with the great Mark Smith. . . ."

6

Jumpstart

*Bioenergy therapy reduces or eliminates
certain symptoms or pains without the use
of drugs and without detrimental side effects.
It is the same as if a car had a low battery
and could not start until it got a jump from
another car's fully energized battery.*

Certainly one thing about my life has been great since
that bout with the sigmoidoscope and surgeon: my health.
I can see the effects that the breath of youth causes not
only on the healed but in the healer. Often I'll be tired and
don't really want to teach class or start a therapy session.
But in just minutes, with deep breathing and calm
visualization, my energy returns. By the end of class or

therapy sessions, my energy is much higher than it was at the start. Sometimes I feel so energized and alive that it is hard to go to bed if the session was held late in the evening; I've even gotten phone calls at 2 or 3 A.M. from people I've just worked on who are themselves so jazzed up they cannot sleep.

A woman who was in my class learning to see auras was also coming to see me for bioenergy therapy. She was very troubled by what she thought was another being who would try to speak through her, most often when she was meditating. As I started to work on her energy field, she would begin this unintelligible, guttural speech and almost seem to float away in a trance. In the first session, I even had to catch her as she began to fall backward.

Talk about not being grounded! But she seemed very sincere and possessed a brilliant purple aura, which usually denotes a very spiritual nature. In her inner field there was also some chartreuse, which is the color of healing, and gold, which is also associated with spirituality, and the colors seemed to be fighting for dominance.

As the classes and sessions progressed, changes were notable. The voice was still there, but she didn't try to float away, and her aura became more stable, settling in on purple and golden colors. But after a session, she was so energized she couldn't fall asleep.

One man who had trouble sleeping due to cancer experienced the opposite effect, however. He was wide awake early one morning, lounging on a couch reading the newspaper, when I started the session. He had just returned home from several days in the hospital, and his wife informed me of his inability to fall asleep. As this was the first time for him, he was alert and curious about the impending therapy session. He asked if he needed to be standing for it. I assured him he could remain on his side, needing only to put down the newspaper and remain relaxed.

He watched me with a curious smile as I started to smooth the aura around his head. Working my way down his chest, I could really feel the enlarged lymph nodes all over his torso, but especially in the groin area. I have no idea why this would have happened so quickly, but the energy seems to have allowed his body to do what it most needed to do, and within a minute or two at most, he was not only sleeping but snoring loudly! His wife covered him with a blanket and later told me he slept until noon, when she was forced to wake him so that he could take his next dose of chemotherapy. His cancer went into complete remission soon after that for several months. Although it would be impossible to claim bioenergy therapy had anything to do with it, at least he was able to sleep soundly after that one session, and his body was able to start healing itself.

This may be the greatest benefit of this type of non-invasive therapy: to reduce or eliminate certain symptoms or pains without detrimental side effects or the use of drugs, so that the body is given the chance to heal itself. It is the same as if a car had a low battery and could not start until it got a jump from another car's fully energized battery.

The energy transfer between human beings appears to be the same. We talk of being cheered up by a visit from a good friend or a letter from a loved one. Taken one step further, this sending of love in close personal proximity, face-to-face, here and now, using these healing techniques, supercharges the body's electrical system.

The effects are the same regardless of any belief (or disbelief) system we may adhere to, and these sometimes dramatic benefits have been witnessed in infants and animals where the belief that they will get better (the so-called placebo effect) cannot possibly be present. Whether we want to or not, the energy is still present and is received when sent, just like a letter from a lover.

What is just as amazing is the health and well-being imparted to the sender. Properly done, this energy transfer happens spontaneously and is merely directed by the sender and channeled in a gentle way to the receiver. A strong feeling of love and wanting to help the person should be the motivating factor, not any egotistical idea that "I" did it. When asked how they achieve their successes, the greatest healers will say "I" had nothing to do with it. The more open and loving the sender, the more this loving energy is allowed to pass through undiluted, and it enhances both participants in a truly wonderful way.

Jumpstarting the Aura

In my aura classes, when a student's energy is seen to be depleted or cloudy gray, we conduct a little experiment. As the subject continues to be viewed by the rest of the class, he or she is told to rub the hands together and place them in front of the body, palms facing up. When I place my hands over the subject's hands about four to six inches above the center of the palm, my hands moving back and forth slowly, the subject will start to feel heat and some slight tingling sensations. Because I am kneeling in front of the person, the aura around his or her head and shoulder area is still visible to the rest of the class.

Within moments, the effects of this jumpstart are readily visible. The aura will grow in size and brightness, often dramatically. Whatever color was present is usually strengthened and often changed to the next higher frequency; for instance, a green aura may start to take on blue or violet characteristics. Sometimes the aura will be "taken over" and mimic whatever color I'm showing at the time. Even after I move my hands away, the aura will continue to show rejuvenation and, once charged, will grow on its own.

You can try it yourself. Start with a basic scan of the auric field and notice its qualities and characteristics. Even if you cannot yet see color, determine the shape, size, and luminance of the aura. If color is visible, watch for any changes in hue and intensity as well as clarity and radiance once the jumpstart occurs.

If there is more than one other person present, you might try to write down your findings individually and compare notes afterward. This also gives you more than one subject to view, and noting the changes between different individuals is a good exercise.

To view a jumpstart, the subjects should stand face-to-face and sideways from the viewer and lightly rub their own hands together for a few seconds. When the subjects place their hands, palms open but not touching, over and under each other's, subtle changes will occur in each person's aura.

In some cases, the aura will appear to be repelled by the other person's aura, almost shrinking away from it; other times, the individuals' auras will actually begin to merge or meld together. If both subjects are asked to think about love or someone that they love, even if it is not the person in front of them, subtle or sometimes dramatic changes occur and are visible immediately. You can try other emotions as well: hate, fear, worry, jealousy, et cetera, with similar immediate (but different) results. Now you can see in the physical body's external auric field the changes brought about by thoughts and emotions.

Once you have practiced seeing the aura enough to spot the halo of each person within a few seconds, you are ready to experiment. Another way of altering another's aura is to place an object on his or her crown chakra. You can use various items such as magnets, crystals, watches, necklaces, or precious stones and place each item on the top of the head of the subject to be viewed.

Breakthroughs for Bioenergy

The ability to visualize the aura is one of those doors that some would not want us to open. Previously considered the private reserve of mystics and clairvoyants, this knowledge was considered dangerous for mass consumption and is still burdened with esoteric or possibly even occult overtones in some circles. But then, until recently, books on something as benign as handwriting analysis were also grouped in the occult section of the Library of Congress! Now both handwriting analysis and studies of the human aura are listed under the heading of psychology.

This occurred when pioneering scientist Shaficia Karagulla, M.D., studied clairvoyant manifestation, or what she called "Higher Sense Perception," in the mid-1960s. Her book, *Breakthrough to Creativity*, describes her scientific background and the methodology used to explore the unknown aspects of the human "super-consciousness." Dr. Karagulla investigated and later witnessed the fantastic experiences of true clairvoyants, some of whom were her fellow physicians. They regularly diagnosed illnesses by touch or inner insight, as well as by "seeing the energy fields around human beings," Dr. Karagulla's description of the aura.

So it is left to science to prove the nature and effects of the human energy field, because with the advent of Kirlian photography in the 1930s, we can no longer dispute the existence of such a field. In these photographs, energy fields are visible as white bands of energy around all types of matter. Further research is being conducted in this country and elsewhere that suggests the importance that these minute electromagnetic fields have within and surrounding the body. Mainstream science, in places such as the Menninger Foundation in Kansas and the National Institute of Health in Maryland, is actively engaged in the study of these bioelectrical phenomena—with some surprising results.

Did you know, for example, that the human body has a hitherto unknown entire network of microscopic nerve fibers that permeate every organ and tissue type? They are chemically connected to the pineal gland, itself a little-known, pea-sized object at the base of the brain. Or did you know that there is measurable electric current in the bloodstream and other tissue not directly related to the nervous system? Until very recently, established medical thinking would not have allowed for the possibility that such things might exist.

These and other recent discoveries suggest that we might not have been as knowledgeable as we thought about the inner workings of the human body. Dr. Harold Moses of Vanderbilt University, the past president of the American Association for Cancer Research, recently said, "What we've learned about cancer . . . in the last ten years is incredible, and eighty percent of that knowledge has been gained in the last five years." He thinks major breakthroughs in the prevention and treatment of cancer are within our grasp in the very near future. It is these studies and others involving the bioenergy field that have jumpstarted our better understanding of disease and its origins.

7

A Healthy Glow

*The energy you exude is the energy
you attract. If you put out a positive vibe,
you tend to attract and surround yourself
with like-minded or positive-vibed people.*

Whatif we were able to gauge our health on a day-to-day basis by what we see as well as what we feel? Not just how we looked physically in the mirror, but how we saw ourselves and how we felt about ourselves? What if you used your newfound auric ability to see how you felt in a whole new way? Up to now, you've been ignoring the most powerful aspect of your physical presentation—the color and radiance of your own aura.

You can see what other people feel about you when you look at your aura in the mirror. They may not be consciously aware that they're sensing it, but that's what so-called good or bad vibes are really all about. And since you now know this little secret, you have the power to change your own auric presentation through good thoughts, emotions, meditation, and prayer.

Coloring Your Aura

The energy you exude is the energy you attract. This is a truism all the way across the board, not just with auric energy. If you put out a positive vibe, you tend to attract and surround yourself with like-minded or positive-vibed people. People who have negative, pessimistic, or cynical energy tend to attract that same kind of energy, creating a kind of self-fulfilling prophecy, if you will. Therefore, the auric envelope that you maintain throughout your life is an instant attraction to similar kinds of auric energies. You know this instinctively when you first meet someone, and as discussed in previous chapters, this has as much to do with the electrical current that you surround yourself with as the chemical makeup of your physical being.

As I travel around the country talking to various groups, I mention a work that is now several years old by Carole Jackson called *Color Me Beautiful* wherein a person, particularly a woman, will dress according to her seasonal coloration. Some women, because of their hair, eye, and skin color, are "summer" women; others may be fall, spring, or winter individuals. This may work for some people, but I find that a large majority say that, in fact, it does not work for them. This has to be because the most important color that you possess—your auric color—is not taken into account.

Those folks who take the time or have the inclination to choose color schemes and surrounding materials that match their own radiant energy field are often among the happiest, most creative and harmonious people that we know. When women tell me that they do not feel comfortable in their assigned season and, in fact, typically look and feel better in other colors than those recommended by the book, they often are surprised when they first see their auric color in the mirror and realize that they own many articles of clothing that are complementary—if not in fact identical—to the color that they exude.

It cannot be overstated how important it is to look at your aura on a daily basis. You will notice changes as the color moves up or down on the color frequency range and, as we have also discussed in other chapters, your health and well-being can be seen in your auric field—but only if you look at it! It does you no good to look at your aura once and then forget about it. It can easily become a daily habit in the morning, as you are preparing yourself to face the day.

You can detect illness before it manifests in the body, and on a happier note, you can also use this auric self-examination to help make your wardrobe selection for the day easier! If you get into the habit of checking out your aura on a daily basis and dressing accordingly, you will find a greater sense of peace and harmony in your daily activities because you will be within the color boundaries set by your auric field.

Some people, however, take color awareness to extremes. Some women I know almost never dress in anything other than black. Others always prefer neutral colors, and some women in particular tend to gravitate toward white, but typically not year-round. It is true, from a practical viewpoint, that white (because of its reflective nature) tends to be a cooler color to wear in the summer, but more and more I notice women and men wearing black even during the hottest months of the year. I have asked several of them why they choose to wear an absorptive color even during the summer months, and the reaction varies slightly but revolves around some expression of comfort, ease, and security in the wearing of black-colored clothing. Perhaps this is a defense mechanism and a way in which to hide your energy field. On the subconscious level, it may be a way to exert more power and influence over your surroundings by having something of a mysterious quality about you, which black can provide.

Remember that you do attract the energy that you exude. Animals use their natural coloration to blend in with the surrounding environment when they are trying to be stealthy, either for survival as a defense against predators or when they are, in fact, predators stalking their prey. It may be some of that basic animal instinct at play in the colors that we choose to adorn ourselves with, whether to attract a mate or to defend ourselves against those who would rob us of our energy or change our basic auric color.

Coloring Your Environment

There is a school of harmonious living that teaches ancient concepts of peace and harmony within our environment. Created thousands of years ago in the Orient, it is known as *feng shui* (literally meaning "wind and water"). The way in which we lay out the buildings we live in—whether they are our homes or offices—and the things that we put in these buildings and rooms have a great deal of consequence in our mental health and long-term well-being.

This sense of living harmoniously within the environments that we find ourselves in also has an application to auras. Once again, the energy that we surround ourselves with tends to be the energy that we ourselves possess, and we tend to reject or repel energy that is not harmonious with who we are and what we represent. It is not too much of a stretch to say that we literally mirror in our environments what we have internalized as far as our thoughts and emotions are concerned. These exterior expressions—particularly insofar as they pertain to colors of clothing or types of furniture—are usually very strong indicators of who we are aurically.

Rolls-Royce Motors, automaker of choice for the queen of England, has an exclusive color, named royal claret, that has a complex combination of colors best described as a dark reddish purple. It is used only for the royal coaches.

England is also the place where color baths and color meditations were quite popular as recently as the first half of this century. Many proponents of these therapies are still around today who claim that by "bathing" in the light projected through large jars of colored water, we derive various therapeutic effects. Thinking of colors or imagining colorful scenes in nature is reputed to have similar effects. Drinking the color-charged water is encouraged by some, as well.

I have not tried working with water, but I do know how effective color meditation can be, especially when trying to relax or to energize the mind.

Have trouble going to sleep? Concentrate on projecting a dark, clear blue—the color of the sky on a cloudless day—on the back of your closed eyelids. If you can hold on to this visualization for ninety seconds or more, you will be very near the Land of Nod, if not already snoring.

Have a tummy ache? Concentrate on a bright, vibrant orange color, and your stomach should settle down.

Want a quick blast of energy and more refreshment than an hour-long nap? Visualize golden yellow entering your whole body as you breathe in deeply, getting rid of dark gray waste as you exhale. Breathe in to a count of four, exhale to a count of four, and relax without inhaling for a count of four before starting the whole process over. If you do this for ten minutes, you will feel wonderfully rejuvenated and as rested as if you had spent ten times as long sleeping.

Colors do play a major role in our lives and affect us in many fundamental ways we may not be aware of. Learning to use color in a whole new way could have a very positive effect on our health and everyday life by leading to improvement that can be seen in your aura and felt in your body.

Auras and Your Health

Just imagine what effects thoughts and emotions cause in our internal physical state! Recent studies by scientific researchers show a strong correlation between our emotional state and our immune system. The relationship between brain-wave activity and pulse rate, body temperature, breath rate, galvanic skin emissions, pupil dilations, gastric flow, and immune response now is well documented.

Can our emotions and thoughts make us sick? Do we think ourselves into dis-ease? Is there some way our bodies get disrupted by negative stress factors, possibly of our own making? The evidence—including the changes you have just seen in the aura—emphatically supports that notion.

Does that mean you can think yourself well? Do you keep yourself healthy on a day-to-day basis without even knowing it consciously? Are prayer and meditation good for us on a physical as well as a mental and spiritual plane? The answer again is emphatically yes!

The power of prayer in the healing process is also well documented. And what is prayer but a concentrated emotional exercise directed with an open and humble heart to a higher being in order to effect a positive change in one's self or others? You are in effect requesting a jumpstart on the cosmic level. The energy you send is amplified through divine intercession when you actively hope and pray for help.

The popular expression "Be careful what you wish for; it might come true" shows how often we do experience success in attaining physical goals through a mental or emotional outpouring. Physical action helps, but "the wish is father to the thought" is another cliché that demonstrates our deep-seated understanding that some tangible things really do have their origins in the intangible realm of the mind. It isn't hard to see the link, then, between the mind and the healing process. The mind and the body are one closed and interlinked system, and one cannot be separated from the other.

Modern medicine tends toward specialization of skills and compartmentalization of treatment. Anyone who has had a recent experience in a hospital knows this frustrating truth. Each separate department will want its own samples of blood, urine, et cetera, even though you just gave samples to another department not half an hour previously. Medical techniques may be wonderful for treating specific symptoms, but where is the healing art needed to maintain the health of the whole person? Yes, we can accomplish miracles with modern medicine, but often in a dehumanizing way, with side effects almost as bad as the illness itself. Treatment of the whole system—body and mind—is ultimately the path we must follow.

This combination of new scientific techniques and old healing arts is in fact happening as the medical community gives grudging acknowledgment and acceptance to many natural folk remedies, previously and disdainfully dismissed as superstitions. Science is proving, for example, that certain foods and natural herbs offer a wide range of medicinal benefits, some curative, others preventive in nature.

The debate over the effects of electromagnetism on the human organism, however it turns out, at least raises the question of whether the use of these "good" technologies such as the television, computer, and cellular phone or even proximity to electric power lines can have a downside of increased incidence of illness, including various cancers. Our health as human beings may be more of a delicate balancing act than previously thought, with a good electrical balance being just as important as a good chemical one.

The recent craze of getting in touch with our bodies and ourselves shows how far we have come from the belief that science can render all necessary remedies to maintain health and that we need only be passive non-participants in the process. "Take a pill" is being replaced with "eat a healthier diet and get some exercise." There is a general feeling of wanting to take back control of our lives, even if we don't know how or why we lost it.

Taking responsibility for our own health is essential. Even though we must rely on the wonders of modern medicine to bail us out when we suffer major trauma, proper self-help may eliminate the need in the first place. When it is time for a coronary bypass, you need the surgeon, but it is better not to need the bypass.

Proper exercise and diet play vital roles in maintaining proper health, but what about proper attitude? Even if we're following an exercise and diet regimen to the letter and taking all the proper vitamins, stress could still kill us. Once again, the mind and the body are a team, totally interactive and cohesive in nature, not some amalgamation of individual systems that operate independently. How we feel is frequently more influenced by our attitude about ourselves, positive or negative, than by any strictly physical condition. And how we feel can often be diagnosed by our auras.

It will take many years, but a time might come when seeing auras will be as commonly practiced and accepted as it seems to have been in antiquity. Wouldn't it be wonderful if we as humans redevelop these skills to the point that we can see when someone tells a lie because the aura suddenly turns a dark shade of green? Or know when someone we love is about to be ill as the aura becomes gray?

Perhaps illness itself will be less prevalent once we become attuned to seeing these subtle electrical changes before the illness has a chance to manifest in the body. With love as the prevailing positive energizer, healing of self and others will become the norm, not the rare exception, through the use of bioenergy transfer.

8

Professional Auras

People all have different types of auras,
showing colors and shapes that can
sometimes be recognizable as belonging
to a specific profession.

Even though everyone's aura is unique, with practice you will begin to see patterns emerge in the colors of similar types of individuals. Teaching in a large classroom environment, and later out in the world, certain students become excellent examples in that they exhibit particular qualities that, with experience, soon became easily assigned to a profession or lifestyle. Engineers, nurses, secretaries, artists, doctors, lawyers, farmers, and musicians all have different types of auras, showing colors and shapes that can sometimes be recognizable as belonging to a specific profession.

Giving Auras the Business

A little game we used to play in class was "pin the profession on the aura." After a brief description of what the color was, and what part of the body each color affected, I would attempt to guess each person's job based on the colors and intensities exhibited.

Some were easy to guess.

Although they never showed up in their scrubs, nurses are almost invariably that very same color, aqua green; this is due to their role as caregivers. One nurse's aura was so green that many people in the audience saw her color immediately and remarked about how uniform and bright its shape and intensity was. She possessed a luminous pastel green aura, but was wearing a brown jacket over a tan sweater. I asked her to remove the jacket to see if that would make any difference, and in fact this did increase, but not change, the color (generally, the less clothing a person is wearing, the easier it is to see the aura).

Knowing that green is the color of balance and healing, centered as it is on the thyroid area in the upper thoracic region, I was not surprised when she admitted that she had been a nurse for eighteen years, with the last six being in private duty at the homes of invalids. Green, in the lighter shades, is always a sign of a harmonious and healing nature and is commonly found in the nursing profession. Green is also considered a neutral color in the spectrum, as it appears between the hot colors of red, orange, and yellow and the cool colors of blue, violet, and purple.

Color is vibration on the visual level, just as musical tones are vibrations registered by the ear. A correlation can be drawn between green and the musical key of F major. Many composers use certain keys to paint a particular musical "color" and think that sound has an effect on the soul. For example, Beethoven's Pastoral Symphony no. 6 is in the key of F. Descriptive titles used for different movements in this symphony, such as "Peasants Picnic in the Fields," show that Beethoven had the color of green grass in mind when he wrote it. Pachelbel's Canon in D, the "sunshine key," is yellow, and it is hard to imagine a brighter or more happy and uplifting piece of music. It is certainly conceivable that these various vibrations do have resonant, or sympathetic, vibrations in different parts of body and soul.

Surprising, then, is the fact that most doctors are dark blue or indigo. At first, you might think that doctors would be even more green than nurses, but if you think about their differing roles in health care, it actually makes sense. Doctors utilize more brain power in their line of endeavor, outsmarting illness or applying some chemical or mechanical fix to the problem. Their method is rigorously taught and tested in a cerebral environment and dispassionately dispensed in hospital operating rooms, where emotions would inhibit their effectiveness. Blue, being the cooler color of the mind and intellect, makes perfect sense for doctors, since so much of their energy is expended in thought. The serious nature of their work can cause an abundance of dark blue or indigo to manifest in their inner aura—colors that are located in the region of the head.

A friend who lived across the street from my little apartment in Georgetown was a young resident surgeon who frequently enthused about the joys of cutting into people. "Any good surgeon loves to cut. You have to really want to do it to be any good at it." He would regale me with various cases and seemed to enjoy watching me squirm as he described in graphic detail some of his operating-room exploits. His aura would appear bright yellow and glow as he got more and more worked up about how he loved to "slash for cash" (his words). I could readily see in his aura how much he enjoyed his work—yellow being the color of joy and vibrancy, affecting the heart and solar plexus region in the body.

Then one day I saw him, and he was uncharacteristically subdued—his aura a heavy gray—and his mood pensive. He had been present at and assisted in the operation of William Casey, the director of the CIA. The operation had not gone as expected. Instead of removing a simple tumor, the team of surgeons had discovered a spreading lymphoma, the bulk of which was located in the brain's speech center, which my friend said they "totally removed."

When I remarked that the *Washington Post* had printed the same day, on the front page, that the operation was a success and that Casey (involved in the Iran-Contra affair) would return to work in two to four weeks, he quietly countered, "He'll never get to testify; in fact, he'll never say another word . . . we took all that part out . . . he'll be dead within six months."

His assessment turned out to be accurate, and I never saw that same joyful yellow aura again. He had become mostly grayish blue, showing lighter colors only when playing Gershwin on the piano. It was as if the seriousness of his profession had begun to wear him down, his supreme self-confidence tempered by the rude intrusion of mortality. Rather than going on to specialize in neurosurgery, which had always been his plan, he remains in general practice today.

Other natural professions for blue individuals are engineering and science. Having worked as a technical recruiter for several years in the defense and aerospace industry, I've been in a wonderful position to view these people. I make it a point to have a white board on the wall behind the interview chair, and I have seen literally thousands of applicants in this environment. Of course, there are exceptions, but in the vast majority, the color that is most prevalent is some shade of blue.

Engineers tend to have a light, almost sky blue color, and this can be very close to the head. Fuzzy or milky in nature, this shows the mind in the process of problem solving. Opaque colors denote unresolved situations or struggle. As the color becomes clearer, a more complete or settled nature is evident. Transparency is a sure sign of attainment of goals or closure in some endeavor. Possibly because they are just beginning their studies and experiments, this clarity is rare, particularly in young scientists and engineers.

Auras in a Box

Not only is the color indicative, but the shape of the aura is related to certain professions as well. Unusual, for all but engineers, is the square, or box, halo.

One of the most dramatic examples of a box halo was witnessed by an entire class, as I had them write down what they saw without any prior commentary on my part. This person had a perfectly square aura, which extended laterally out the left side of the head and was dark blue in color. As the class began to see it, murmurs and exclamations could be heard throughout the room. I shushed them and told them to draw or write about what they saw.

Fully three-quarters of the nearly sixty people in the room had drawn the box coming out the left side of the head and written that the color was blue or violet. There was no surprise when the subject said he was the head of an architectural firm in Washington. He certainly had geometric shapes firmly in mind that night!

The only other box shape I've seen that was so perfectly angular belongs to my teacher, Mietek Wirkus. His is actually two boxes. The smaller one, close to the left side of his head, extends three or four inches above the center and proceeds across the top of his head in a straight line out about one foot on the side. The second, much bigger box rises in a straight line, perhaps two feet above the centerline of his head, and extends out the right side.

I have never seen an aura like this before or since, and it is very unusual because most auras are rounded and conform more or less to the outline of the body. The color was what you would expect for a healer, though: golden green or chartreuse, and solidly vibrant.

I don't know what these shapes mean. Maybe they have to do with special gifts or unique brain-wave activity. Perhaps caused by some injury or physical quirk, they are notable in their extreme rarity; however, the individuals show no outward signs of abnormality. Also peculiar is the fact that I've only seen them on people involved in the engineering profession, with the sole exception of my teacher. The triangle, or dunce cap, is far less rare but also somewhat unusual. This was seen numerous times in class and usually seems to be either golden or violet/purple in color. No pattern of lifestyle or professional association is apparent, although some subjects report higher than normal awareness of spiritual matters or psychic phenomena.

I have been told by some of my students that I appear on occasion to have a triangular light above my head, or sometimes rays of light pointing up in a wedge shape or inverted triangle. This triangle shape is most often noted in my auric field when I'm rested and unstressed, frequently right after an extended prayer or meditation period. Colors seem more vibrant at that time as well, tending toward bright yellow or gold in the etheric (inner) aura and purple in the astral (secondary) field.

Standing in front of the class, breathing deeply and thinking loving thoughts, I can feel the warmth spreading throughout my body, with a tingling sensation shooting up my spine, energizing my hands and head. As this rush of energy develops, some members of the

Auras

class will start to remark about shapes or rays of golden or silver light seen extending far above and around my body. When the feelings start to subside, often someone will remark at that moment how the "light has been turned off," and the aura changes shape or color and reverts "back to normal."

Whatever that is.

9

Spiritual Auras

The basic talent allowing us to see an aura is in all of us. In fact, we see auras all the time but are just not consciously aware of the fact.

On one occasion when a friend was viewing my aura, she remarked about "balls of light—golden light—hovering" above my head and over my shoulders. On another occasion, she says she saw "luminous figures—spirit guides, I think—but definitely three beings on either side and behind" me. During yet another viewing some months later, she was sure she saw "the outline of a figure—very large—directly in back of and surrounding" my image.

I finally asked her what these figures meant, and whether this was not unusual, since she often said she saw beings around me. "Not unusual for you, it seems; I see them around many people."

Her answer startled me, because I had never witnessed these phenomena in other people. And now she was telling me she saw them all the time!

I didn't know what to make of all this. It is possible that she is clairvoyant and that truly clairvoyant people just see these figures as a matter of course. She wasn't surprised or perturbed by their appearance, calling them "spirit guides" at one point. And since I remember seeing "guardian angels" as a child, perhaps I shouldn't be too worried. Maybe this is another natural talent we all have at birth that gets lost or forgotten as we become culturally and societally indoctrinated. Clairvoyance might be a "remembrance" of these lost natural powers that reside in some of us more readily than others.

What I do know is that the basic talent allowing us to see an aura is still in all of us. In fact, we see auras all the time but are just not consciously aware of the fact. It is only when we turn off the rational, cognitive part of our brain that we can let the intuitive part "see" the human energy field. Colors (and certainly other beings) will not be visible to everyone, but I have never met anyone who could not at least see the field around the head and shoulders after a minute or two of practicing the techniques while viewing one or two subjects in the proper light.

Even under less-than-optimum conditions (neon or fluorescent light, patterned or colored wallpaper background, too close proximity to the subject), a majority of first timers will still see something.

Frequently, I have proven this to skeptics who—like myself many years ago—don't believe this is possible. We'll pick out a person seated some distance away at a restaurant or in a public place and, without being too obvious, "unfocus" on their aura. While not always successful, it works more often than not.

This is much easier to do in a classroom environment, where the aura will be easier to see with better lighting and a more conducive viewing background.

Plant Auras

My clairvoyant friend is a truly gifted woman who has been aware of auras for over thirty years. She started by studying plants, developing a keen sense of awareness by using small, dense plants and shrubs as her subjects. A plant's field is very stationary and uniform and, although more subtle than human's auras, easy to see.

Try it.

Place a healthy, small plant on a table near a light. Once again, you must focus past the plant, either on another part of the table or on a wall behind it. You should notice a fuzzy, light green envelope around the outline where leaves and air meet. The more dense and healthy the plant, the brighter, and therefore easier to see, the aura.

It is also fun to see the effect of various substances placed in the plant's proximity. Once you have established a base line aura, try placing a thin glass of red wine very near, but not in, the plant's field. Within a minute or two, you should notice more vibrancy and some growth in the auric field of the plant. It might actually appear to reach out and touch the glass, as if the plant wanted to drink! Unless the plant is very dry, this won't happen if the glass is filled just with water. Try placing anything magnetic near the plant, and you'll see an opposite effect. Most metallic substances also will cause a similar but lessened "turning away" by the plant. This is the same reaction we see in human auras when confronted with these objects. If the magnetic force is strong enough, the aura will be completely "devoured" and totally disappear!

Plants can also be useful as practice objects for viewing when people aren't around. My friend who learned how to see auras by viewing plants swears that this is the easiest and best way to learn. She has one of the most developed abilities in aura reading that I've ever encountered, so who am I to argue with success? Perhaps having actively used this talent for more than thirty years also plays a part in enhancing her remarkable ability, but she still spends time viewing various plants as well as people.

Holy Auras

Church is also likely to provide a peaceful viewing environment, and as the sermon is being delivered, you should have a wonderful opportunity to see rays or fully energized fields around the speaker, especially if the talk is devoutly delivered. People called to the priesthood should have spiritual characteristics that manifest in the aura. Truly religious ones, no matter what denomination or faith, will show colors higher up on the frequency scale, usually indigo, violet, or purple. Gold or silver will be frequently mixed in as well. Remember that depictions of holy people throughout every culture have large bright silver or gold halos, never red, brown, green, or black.

Why, then, do priests traditionally wear black? There are both good theological and practical reasons based on wanting to appear humble, unworldly, and above any concern for fashion or the "glorification of the flesh." The concerns of the priest should focus on the life of the spirit and be open to its call. Black itself is not a color per se, but rather the absence of color, and it is absorptive in nature, reflecting or resonating back no particular hue, showing no preference. On both the metaphorical and metaphysical levels, black is ideal for one who prays daily, "Lord, fill me with Thy blessing . . . for Thou art the Light of the World." *Lux aeterna luceat eis*—let perpetual light shine upon them.

What about colors in priestly vestments? At different times of the year and on certain feast days, one particular color is used exclusively for that day. For example, red is reserved for martyrs' feast days and Pentecost, when Christ ascended into heaven and flames appeared over the heads of the apostles. White is for the most important events in the liturgical calendar: Easter and Christmas. Purple is used during Advent (before Christmas) and Lent, the time of self-denial before Christ's resurrection (Easter). Green is used during the balance of the year and is the color normally seen. These colors have been used in Christian worship for almost one thousand years, and this did not happen by accident.

Historically, purple has been reserved for the robes of the higher ranks in the Catholic Church and European royalty. Being "drawn toward the purple" is a very old expression denoting aspirations of upward mobility in those two hierarchic institutions. One of my Jesuit teachers of philosophy left the order abruptly but remained a priest so that he might follow his call to the purple, feeling pastoral duties, not teaching, would lead him more quickly up the ladder.

Once again, we see that color is used for a variety of purposes in life, and never should be taken for granted. The spiritual nature and effect of certain colors on the aura, especially the higher vibrational ones such as violet, indigo, and purple, have been well-known for millennia. When these colors are predominant in a person's aura, it's a safe bet you are looking at a spiritually attuned individual.

10

Charisma

"Some are born great, some achieve greatness, and some have greatness thrust upon them," but Shakespeare could just as easily have described the various ways one might attain charisma.

As my ability to see auras has expanded over time, so too has my portfolio of interesting subjects. Having been a performing artist for almost half of my life, I worked with many famous people and came in direct contact with those reputed to possess the rarest of gifts: charisma.

What is charisma?

How do you describe it?

Who has it, and how do you get it?

Some people say it is animal magnetism. Others might describe it as physical attractiveness coupled with a charged and outgoing personality. Still others might not mention physical characteristics at all but talk about a commanding presence that transcends personality and pulchritude.

But everyone agrees that certain people just have it, and that you'll know it when you see it.

What do the auras of such people look like? First, not only are all charismatic people unique and not necessarily famous, but not all famous people have charisma. "Some are born great, some achieve greatness, and some have greatness thrust upon them," but Shakespeare could just as easily have described the various ways one might attain charisma. There is no set pattern or color similar to what I've noticed in other groups of people (e.g., engineers and nurses); each in some way exhibits a power or control over themselves and others. This usually goes beyond sheer ego and should not be confused with charisma, which registers much lower in energy and color.

Some families have several members, each of whom exhibits some form of this special gift. I've had the opportunity to view such a family with all these gifts in one place and at one time, spread across three generations: Janet Auchincloss; her daughter, the late Jackie Onassis; and her granddaughter, Caroline Kennedy.

Almost by accident, I happened to be present at a family gathering to celebrate the christening of Janet Auchincloss's great-grandniece Alexandra at the Yellow

House at Hammersmith Farm in Newport, Rhode Island, during the America's Cup races in the late summer of 1983.

One of three non–family members present in a group of about two dozen, I was the guest of Jamie Auchincloss, whom I knew through a mutual friend in Washington, D.C. This friend, myself, and the priest who performed the baptism were given a rare glimpse inside their world, and during the course of the day, I was able to observe the similarities and differences among these women in a variety of settings.

I was to perform at the gathering after the ceremony but due to complications was merely a guest all that day at the house and later that afternoon at their private beach. I was invited back to perform for a large outdoor picnic three days later, giving me another opportunity to view them and many others, royalty included.

That day of the christening, however, turned out to be the perfect environment in which to watch three generations of great women. Since I didn't have to work the party, I was free to meet and observe them at home in a very relaxed environment—so relaxed, in fact, that I saw Jackie, with "greatness thrust upon" her, thrust a piece of christening cake into her sister Lee's face as one was being smashed into her own, both women laughing and screaming like schoolgirls.

As they regained their composure, the differences in auras between them was striking: Jackie by far the more radiant, Lee more reserved and darker. If anything, Lee showed more ego, and Jackie more charisma. There was a shadowy darkness surrounding Lee that seemed totally absent from her sister. This was contrary to what one might assume, knowing the historical facts surrounding Jackie, but she was yellow, gold, and pink alternating with purple, all quite bright and clear in tone.

The kaleidoscopic nature of her aura that day was most impressive and denotes a very complex yet goodhearted person. There were elements of shyness (pink) coupled with strong religious reserves (purple), supported by an intrinsic sense of love and caring (yellow) and high personal attainment with control mentally, emotionally, and spiritually (gold).

On the personal level, Jackie was somewhat abstract and distant, much like her daughter. As Caroline lay reclining on the patio chaise longue near the corner of the house, off by herself observing the gathering, she seemed very ethereal. I remember how translucent she looked, in a way almost ghostly, with pastel colors surrounding her head and shoulders in a tight chartreuse and pale blue band. Whereas her mother's eyes were constantly changing, never fixing her gaze too long on one spot, Caroline had a steady, penetrating look of intelligence and total composure. But she, too, seemed remote.

For at least half an hour, she remained undisturbed, and I couldn't help but glance over frequently, fighting the urge to walk over and talk to her. She had charisma all right, but it almost seemed to trap her in a crystalline shell, isolating her and discouraging any approach.

My friend—who for many years had openly talked of meeting her and fantasized about marrying her in order that together they might rekindle Camelot—was frozen in his tracks, unable to approach the object of so many of his desires. He is not normally the retiring type, having been a Green Beret A-team commander in Vietnam and a survivor of polio. Such was Caroline's power of presence, however, that he and I and everyone else there kept a respectful distance even after she arose and went into the house. I saw her talk only to her aunt and grandmother, for whom she seemed to have a great love.

But who couldn't love Janet? So accessible, warm, and gracious, she made me feel I was truly welcome and seemed genuinely interested in me and my musical career. Having achieved greatness through a series of marriages to famous and powerful men, and having given birth to arguably the most admired woman on the planet, Janet Auchincloss was the matriarch of all she surveyed that day and was herself a fascinating study.

She possessed an amber and orangish aura that shows vitality and physical energy coupled with a warm personality. There was also a golden glow that seemed to spread around her and extended quite far into the room. To a greater degree than anyone else there, she drew people toward her with this soft and comforting radiance.

Surrounded by family, standing near the back door leading to the patio with the soft afternoon light illuminating her, Janet seemed almost regal in composure, and I was struck with the feeling that she came from a different age and belonged to a different time. Perhaps in later years her progeny will take on this same aura of supreme generosity and placid majesty, but on this day, at least, her aura was unsurpassed in grace and true charisma.

Comparing their auric personalities shows Jackie to be the most complex, exhibiting fire and brilliance with many colorful facets, much like a diamond. She was also the most mercurial, but in a totally controlled way. Caroline was intelligent, reserved, placid, and composed, with lots of higher-level energy held in check. She exuded a quiet and cool demeanor that was in no way snooty, but somehow failed to ignite any desire for closeness, and was the least approachable person in that group. Janet was just the opposite, perhaps because this was her house and she was most in her element, surrounded by her brood on a beautiful day celebrating a joyous occasion.

All three were quite different, but each one in her own way practically defined the term *charisma*.

There are also famous people whom I have met who are not particularly charismatic. Some European royalty I met at parties the following week fit that description. Prince Michael of Kent was a very down-to-earth sort of fellow—that is, after he got out of his hot-air balloon! He seemed quite normal and approachable, with a ruddy brown and orange aura. This shows a strong physical capability and is tied to the second chakra, which is important for the physical health and well-being of the body. I was introduced to him just before I began to perform but didn't note any special magnetism at that time.

The late Prince Johannes Thurn-und-Taxis of Bavaria was also less than electric when we met at the picnic on the hill of Hammersmith Farm, overlooking the sailing ships. I saw him on three occasions that week at America's Cup parties in Newport and was invited to play aboard his yacht for one of them. At no time did he display anything remotely resembling charisma, but rather seemed decadent and egotistic. It was very hard to see any aura at all on him, but what was there was very dark and broken, close to the body, and dull. This is the same type of aura one can see on a depressed or chemically dependent person, someone with the weight of the world on his shoulders. Perhaps he was physically ill and taking some form of medication, which can greatly affect the aura in a negative way.

Certainly the mood was festive onboard the yacht the night of his party, with many glittery people in tuxedos and fancy ball gowns running around in their stockinged feet so as not to mar the bleached teak deck. People seemed to be having the time of their lives as I walked around strumming my guitar and taking requests in my own stockinged feet.

Stopping at one table to play a request from a beautiful young woman, I was quite intrigued by her fiery aura. The lights were soft candles, and the background was a freshly painted white bulkhead, so the aura was easily seen. I found out later that the woman was

Princess Gloria, Thurn-und-Taxis's wife. She was reputed to have as much royal lineage as Prince Johannes and was quite young and beautiful. Later we talked briefly, and she was surprisingly up-to-date on the American music scene, requesting several songs that I was happy to play for her.

Her aura, which I vividly remember, was like a candy cane, with each of the different colors banded together. This type of aura is rarely seen, usually appearing in children or teenagers of European ancestry, sometimes in adults of pure African or Indian stock. I've seen it in white adult males only three times, but never before that night in a white adult female.

That she was female was never in question, being the belle of the ball well into the early hours. I saw her again later that week at a dinner party hosted by "Foxy" Carter, then CIA director of operations in Southeast Asia, at their home in Newport. She was only slightly less vibrant than she had been the night on the yacht, but as I was busy entertaining, I had far less opportunity to study her in depth.

Princess Gloria, perhaps due to her youthfulness and sizable age difference with Prince Johannes, possesses quite a vibrant and unique aura. She is the only person of royal lineage I have seen who displayed characteristics that could be called charismatic.

It is important to reiterate that fame and charisma don't always go hand in hand. There must have been at least one person known to you at some time in your life—be it a teacher or schoolmate, perhaps someone you work with—who displays this quality. In almost every case, these individuals will not have had an instantly recognizable public profile, but this in no way diminishes the gift they so readily display.

11

Auras in Performance

*Some entertainers that I've worked
with are all but unrecognizable offstage.
But put them in lights in front of
thousands of adoring fans, and a
stunning transformation occurs.*

What is the magic of performance? Why do we want to be near it, to watch it, and therefore to take part in it? What makes one performance great and another only average? Could it be some subtle exchange of energy present in one, missing in another? Does the aura of the performer actually touch the audience?

Janis Joplin compared performing to sex—only she thought performing onstage was better! I can tell you from a performer's viewpoint that there are times when I am so in touch with an audience that feelings very similar to postcoital euphoria engulf me as the waves of applause build and crest, crashing down around me. "I had that audience in the palm of my hand" must have been said by every performer who ever stood in front of an audience more than once and liked it. Being onstage is either a terrifying experience you never want to repeat or a tremendous excitement you can never forget. It all depends on forging a loving link with the audience.

A good entertainer lifts our spirits and makes us forget about our personal problems for a while. Whether the medium is music, drama, dance, or even storytelling around a campfire, the audience is drawn into the artist's world. Magic happens when the spell is cast and the artist and audience create a world together. In transcending ordinary, everyday reality, artist and audience create a group aura that might be seen if you could get far enough away to view the group as a whole, but is definitely felt by all present.

One type of performing artist who relies totally on making and holding an immediate and personal link with the audience is the comedian.

When the vibes don't click, it is a very painful experience for artist and audience. Usually the comedian has no place to hide, no instrument to stand behind, no song to sing—just jokes to tell that aren't very funny. Those same jokes told by another person might well be hysterically funny, but only if the auric link is established with the audience first.

Even when he was just starting out as a stand-up comedian, Yakov Smirnoff had already learned this lesson naturally. A recent immigrant from what was then Soviet Russia, he learned the English language as a dishwasher at clubs in the Catskills by listening to the comedians' routines. His accent and timing were terrible, but I immediately liked something about him—his stage presence and willingness to try.

During a weekend spent sharing the stage at a comedy club in Washington, D.C., I got to watch him hone his craft long before he was the star of his own TV show. With childlike wonder and honesty, he was still in a fresh state of cultural shock about everything American. His humor derived from his own experiences both here and in Russia, so audiences generally were tolerant because of his honestly charming excitement that carried them along into his world. By humorously casting his life's tribulations, he held up a mirror in which we viewed both his and our own experiences, but he made us see our world with his Russian eyes. Yakov's real talent is the ability to create that empathy with an audience that transcends cultural, language, and national barriers, and he turns those tremendous potential handicaps into valuable opportunities for unity with his audience.

Every great artist presents a truth. The truth might not always be beautiful, nor will it always be immediately recognized, but when truth and beauty do come together, an ecstatic moment occurs. Ecstasy's Greek root *(ek histemi)* means literally "knocked out of one's stance," or roughly in today's vernacular, "blown away."

Perhaps the truth can set you free in more ways than one.

Almost always, the best art has some elements of the body, mind, heart, and soul present in it, no matter what the format. It draws us out of ourselves and pushes us toward a higher state of awareness and understanding by resonating with some (or all) of these aspects of our true nature. Affirmation of this nature, especially when it touches the heart and soul, is the great attraction to all manner of performing arts. Confirmation of these "ecstatic" moments is what brings us back time after time to relive the magic of this transcendent experience. Both artist and audience are fed and nurtured by this symbiotic relationship.

These empowering experiences certainly are what keep the entertainer and audience coming back for more and may account for some artists' incredible longevity. Comedians such as Bob Hope and Henny Youngman are in their nineties, and George Burns made it to 100—living proof that laughter can keep you young. Famous symphonic conductors as a group are notorious for their long lives, frequently directing orchestras well into their eighties. Only when performers smoke themselves to death (Leonard Bernstein, John Wayne) or drug themselves into oblivion (too numerous to mention) do we see less-than-average life spans in public performers.

So what is this energy transfer that happens onstage? We can see and feel the effects no matter what side of the stage lights we are on. Is the lack of this energy what causes so many performers to indulge in artificial stimulants?

Some lucky stars, like James Taylor, live through their indulgences and perform at or above the level they displayed when first becoming famous, attaining a peace and tranquillity along the way, surprising even themselves. Could the love and adulation they received from so many souls over such a long time have been their real saving grace?

Auras On- and Offstage

In the backstage parking lot, standing between two tractor-trailer rigs and wearing cutoffs and a white t-shirt, a tall, gangly man was blocking my way. His long arms were spread straight out, each palm flat against the aluminum side of one of the trucks, in what could have been a menacing pose were it not for his goofy grin and flamingo-like stance.

"What's in the case?" he asked with apparent interest.

"Damn," I thought, "another nosy roadie, and all I want to do is get backstage and set up." I was late for sound check and didn't have time to show off my custom built guitar to another grungy stagehand. But he wasn't moving to let me pass, and now more than halfway down the tunnel formed by the two long trailers, I put the case down and opened the lid. We both dropped down to one knee as I carefully withdrew the instrument and handed it to him.

"I've never seen anything like this before. What is it? Did you make this?" It was the typical reaction whenever anyone at all interested in musical instruments first sees an A. B. Adams acoustic guitar. Frankly, I sometimes get tired of repeating the litany of all the wonderful details concerning its construction.

But he persisted. "What kind of neck is this? How did he cut it so thin? Look at that inlay. Wow! What are those diagonal braces inside the sound hole for? Does it have a pickup?"

I was really getting impatient and was about to take the guitar out of his hands when he finally coaxed the first chords out of it. We had been no more than three feet apart for perhaps two minutes, but it was not until this moment of musical epiphany that it slowly dawned on me that this was none other than the man who had been on the cover of *Time*. He was the maker of some of my favorite music. In fact, I knew how to play almost all of his songs by heart and owned every one of his records. I'd looked at his face on the covers of records and magazines for years. And yet I'd had no idea that this unpretentious and gentle guy kneeling next to me was James Taylor until he started to play my guitar in his signature style.

Maybe my first impression was misguided by how and where he was standing and by what he wore. It might have been due to my own focus and concentration or nervousness. The expectations of what he would be like after all those years of knowing him only through his music could have played a part, too.

But the fact was, his offstage personality and demeanor, or vibe, were more like that of a roadie or stagehand than that of the internationally renowned rock star and founder of the singer-songwriter movement that he, in fact, was. Rather than projecting energy, he seemed to be internalizing his forces and was on the shy side. This held true each of the subsequent times that I saw him, and although his mood was changeable, occasionally edging toward somewhat somber, he was unfailingly gracious.

On this first meeting, however, he was incredibly open and enthusiastic, telling me many personal anecdotes and asking me for advice on topics such as marriage and children. He alluded to an impending divorce, which shocked me, since the whole world at that time believed his union with Carly Simon was firmly entrenched. Even *Parade* magazine proclaimed on its cover some months later that his "dark night of the soul" had ended, James having been saved from his destructive tendencies by his wife, with whom he was totally in love, and by the responsibilities of raising a family together.

Here I was, feeling like I was on assignment for *Rolling Stone*, except I wasn't asking any questions. He was voluntarily opening his heart and mind to me, a total stranger. That he was entrusting me with his knowledge was more than a little overwhelming, and I'm sorry to say I never really focused on his aura during that time backstage right before the concert.

Quite a different personality emerged once he entered the spotlight, and I was able to study him in detail from that point forward. Much more physically active onstage than I would have guessed, he seemed to draw energy from the members of his band at first, and the music just flowed out of him. As the concert progressed, he became more engaged with the audience, talking more between songs. Calls from the audience of "Where's Carly?" were finally answered, almost painfully, with "ah, she's not . . . ah . . . here." Then he launched into the next song full force, continuing to raise the tempo through three encores.

To say he was wired after the show would be an understatement. This wasn't due to any artificial stimulants (certainly I saw none used), but rather to a natural euphoria that carried on well into the next morning in the hotel lounge, where he played piano and jammed with the other musicians. This was also my first real opportunity to see his aura, and it proved to be a base line for comparison in future encounters.

James Taylor's aura was very dark blue to begin with and proceeded to deepen to violet whenever he became quiet or pensive. Close to the body and quite difficult to see during these times, the energy was all drawn in. Quite thoughtful and shy, he nonetheless exhibited flashes of yellow and purple as he spoke and became animated when something caught his interest.

It was the color green, however, that he most often exemplified, both on- and offstage after a performance. His clear, medium green color was augmented by a golden band when he was comfortably in the midst of singing his songs—whether in front of thousands of people or with just a few in a private setting. Green is the color of healing and balance, and perhaps this shows the therapeutic effect of his music on his own psyche.

He exhibits multiple colors of the spectrum at other times and has a complex auric field. Therefore, it could be surmised that he is most happy and balanced when he's in a musical mode. Words such as "warm," "smoothing," and "mellow" come to mind when one thinks of his music, far different from the well-documented lifestyle of drugs and depressions that were central elements early in his life. Music undoubtedly played a role in overcoming these handicaps, and in recent years he appears to be healthy.

I could also compare his aura with that of his brother Livingston, whom I had known for five years previous to meeting James. The brothers were close in age, and both played and sang their own songs, but at that time they were not all that close personally, Livingston perhaps feeling the burden of constantly being compared with his more famous older brother. A fine songwriter in his own right, it must have been difficult for Liv to hear audiences requesting that he play songs written by James, as they too often did back in the early 1970s.

Although they shared some familiar traits physically, here was an example of two musical brothers with similar styles but very different presentations. Their differences were readily seen in their auras and expressed in their personalities both on- and offstage. Perhaps this could help explain my lack of immediate recognition when I first met James, since my long relationship with Livingston might have preconditioned my expectations that their vibes would be more akin to each other than they turned out to be.

Whereas Livingston was gentle offstage, with a light blue, evenly balanced aura, he assumed a silver sparkle when he played and sang. This was changeable depending on the instrument he was playing or the song he was singing. On piano, blue became more predominant and the silver less bright, perhaps because he was less comfortable on that instrument and had to think more about technique than when he played guitar. If you remember that blue is the color of mental energy, this reaction to increased mental activity or stress is normal and easily explained.

You might want to try this little test on yourself. Once you become comfortable with seeing your own auric colors in the mirror, think of the multiplication tables starting with the number six and proceeding up to the number twelve. As you work harder to remember (or figure out) the answers, notice the difference in color, size, and intensity of your energy field. Unless you happen to be an arithmetic whiz, this should darken, shrink, and lessen the intensity of your visible auric field.

Try it with someone for whom you have already established an auric base line, and the same results should occur. You might even see the color change to blue if the normal base line color is relative to it on the frequency scale (green or violet). If there is blue already in the aura, an effect similar to the one seen in Livingston Taylor's performance aura should be visible.

Another great performer and longtime survivor on the rock-and-roller coaster is the late Jerry Garcia of the Grateful Dead. Despite several near misses over the years, he managed to avoid incorporating himself too literally with the name of his band and flourished on several levels. Making a name for himself in the art world, along with marketing a line of designer apparel items, he showed himself to be a man of colors as well as sounds. Certainly he led a very colorful life—and he had the aura to prove it!

Gregarious and self-effacing, with a strong sense of humor that created an underlying mirthful ambiance whenever I saw him, Jerry also possessed surprising drive and intelligence. All these elements made for a complexity of aura not easy to isolate or define, and I observed such a variety of auric patterns with him that it was difficult to know what was real and what was chemically induced.

When I first met him in New Haven, Connecticut, in 1978, backstage before a Grateful Dead concert, he seemed almost contemplative and subdued. There were sparks of random energy coming off his head and shoulders as he stood in a corner of the large dressing room warming up, waiting to go on. But the gray paint on the cinder-block walls of the coliseum and overhead fluorescent lighting weren't ideal conditions for color determinations, and there were other members of the band I was being introduced to, including Bob Weir, the other guitarist in the band, that prevented me from fully focusing on Garcia.

Back in the hotel room later that night, I got a much better look at Garcia, Weir, and other members of the band and retinue. Here again was perhaps a distorted picture due to the unknown influences of various substances, but both Garcia and Weir showed strongly different vibes in their auras.

Quite complementary in their divergence, Jerry Garcia possessed a more wide-open and colorful field, while Bob Weir had a more controlled and angular aura. Whereas Garcia filled a larger space with a brighter, more electric and eclectic series of colors, Weir was more monochromatic and diffuse.

Weir's aura had a quieter, softer radiance, showing a steely blue gray color and a close projection off the body. Fuzzy in nature but with clearly defined boundaries, his aura brought to mind words such as "cautious," "controlled," and "analytical." He seemed to be quite thoughtful, and he expressed himself in a hesitant yet concise and logical fashion, very similar indeed to his auric presentation, which mirrored the man precisely.

At other times, I've seen him physically quite active and almost out of control, taken to sudden bursts of energy, as if he were breaking out of some form of confinement. I haven't been able to get a steady read on his aura at these times due to such active movement, so I can't tell what color, if any, it changes into, but following such activity, his aura becomes more open and vibrant, with lots of yellow (high emotions) in place of the blue.

Certainly Weir exhibits more energy onstage than Garcia, moving around quite freely while Jerry seemed rooted in one spot, content to let the music do all the movement. It is as if Weir is consciously working to physically overcome his basic auric nature, which is conservative and tightly held, and Garcia was concentrating on marshaling his more free-form and expansive energies into a clearly defined focus—both fighting their own natural tendencies when they played.

This held true when both men were fronting their own personal groups as well, but to a lesser extent. Having performed as the solo opening act for Weir's band Bobby and the Midnights and Jerry Garcia's band Reconstruction, I've been with each of them in several different venues where they have performed as individuals without the frenzy of a complete Grateful Dead experience, although some aspects of it are present whenever they play.

Because I was never a Dead Head, as their followers call themselves, I got an objective look into this colorful and unique lifestyle. A direct carryover of the late 1960s—complete with tie-dyed clothes and psychedelic behavior—this time-warped world was still populated by eighteen-year-olds (some as old as sixty) for whom peace and love were still paramount. Garcia and Weir played off this energy (and each other) in a way that created a sum much greater than their individual parts, driving and being carried along with their faithful fans as they played.

This synergy was totally absent when each man performed separately. Lacking this friendly friction, I always felt a hollowness in their individual efforts, masked somewhat by the ever-present adoring fans but never able to take the energy into that magical realm reserved, it seems, for full communion with the Dead.

Judy Collins, a 1960s-era survivor herself, best known for singing "Amazing Grace" at President Clinton's first inauguration, might tell you that her communion with fans over the years has sustained her own performance aura. She will tell you that "Amazing Grace" is her favorite and most requested song. It has special meaning, not only for civil rights activists who used it as an anthem, but for all the survivors of that socially and politically charged time.

When I first met her as she was about to play at St. Joseph's College in the autumn of 1972, she was radiant, laughing, friendly, and open. We played guitar together backstage before the concert, and she seemed not to have a care in the world. Full of energy, she epitomized the hopes and aspirations of the new generation.

How different Judy looked as she walked in the stage door and trudged down the hallway to her dressing room in late January 1993. Tiny, withdrawn, and quiet, eyes darting, then averting, she looked like a trapped elf. Once again, I didn't recognize someone I thought I knew.

But what a transformation when Judy "Amazing Grace" Collins hit the lights! She went from negative aura to full ecstasy faster than anyone I've ever seen. Could this really be the same person? Clearly the audience had a profound impact on her, and after the concert she radiated a silver sparkle with intermittent rays projecting almost a foot around her head and shoulders.

She talked about being "on a pink cloud" at the inauguration, surrounded as she was by her musical contemporaries and at the head of that class. Different from a quarter century before (If you remember the sixties . . . you weren't there), this was a drug-free, defining moment for her entire generation and one never to be forgotten.

Judging by her radiant aura, she had come full circle with youthful idealism, and at least for that instant, Judy Collins was in the midst of a historic lovefest once again, not at Woodstock this time, but at the White House in Washington for a command performance by her biggest fan, the newly elected president of the United States, Bill Clinton.

It's hard to imagine a more wonderful feeling.

12

Politically Correct Auras

*The auras of politicians tend to be
very different from those of entertainers.
When giving a speech, a politician is
performing and subject to the audience-
actor dynamic, but that is where
the similarity ends.*

Imagine what the late Virginia Kelly, Bill Clinton's mother, must have felt at that moment! Having just seen her son sworn in as the forty-second president of the United States, I saw her as she was flying home to Arkansas early Sunday morning after a week of inaugural festivities that left her on cloud nine. In fact, from what I could see, she might not have needed the airplane!

Sitting across the aisle from her on flight 1661 to Nashville, I had no idea who this woman in black was. She certainly seemed well known to everyone else, shaking hands and signing autographs as she walked up and down the aisle right after takeoff. Maybe she was a country-and-western singer I didn't recognize. The man next to me took a large ceramic tile button with Clinton's picture on it out of his pocket and handed it to me.

"Give this to Virginia when she comes back to sit down. I don't think she's got one of these."

Obviously I was still oblivious, so he said helpfully, "She's the president's mother, you know."

Because this was a regular commercial flight and I assumed it would be unthinkable for the president's mother not to be on Air Force One or some private jet, I honestly wondered why everyone was making such a fuss over the mother of the president—of what—American Airlines?

Only when the captain said in the loudspeaker, "We'd like to thank the Little Rock Mafia for flying home with us today," as applause and cheers rang throughout the cabin, did reality finally dawn on me. Seems I got myself booked on the homebound Arkansas inaugural party junket by accident, and as Virginia came back to her seat, I dutifully handed her the trinket with her son's photograph emblazoned on it.

"That's my boy! That's my boy!" she squealed. "Where did you get this?" I pointed to the man on my left. "Say, I know you, you're Jane's husband!" With that, she put her left hand on my shoulder, bracing herself with her other hand on the top of the seat in front of me, and leaned over six inches in front of my face to commence an animated conversation with Jane's husband. I was up close and personal with the mother of the president, and there were a lot of questions I wanted to ask her. I mumbled something about performing for the Gore family the night before the vice presidential debates and added, "My brother Michael went to school with your son Bill at Georgetown."

"Well, I just knew you were somebody!" she said as she squeezed my shoulder a little harder. Then I finally got to ask my most pressing question, "What does all this really feel like for you?"

Virginia rolled her eyes, tilted her head back, and let out a yelp. Then she looked right at me and, with a beatific smile that permeated her whole being, said slowly with an almost mystical passion, "ohhhh honey. . . ." Words could not describe it; none in fact were necessary. Her look said it all—this was a truly transcendent moment.

How odd, then, that I sensed all was not well with her physically. You might think, with all the peak life experiences happening for her and all the obvious external joy and excitement, that Virginia Kelly's aura would be astounding. Unfortunately, was not the case.

Staying close to her body with very fuzzy and vague pastel colors, her aura showed low vibrancy but a fair degree of luminosity. The color alternated from a dull, burnt range to a very light, frosty blue. Sometimes the aura seemed to vanish entirely, as if the plug had been pulled suddenly. Then, just as suddenly, it would return, glow strongly, flicker, and subside, never extending more than an inch or two out from her body.

At the time, my thoughts were that she must be exhausted from so much excitement, and I was concerned about her sudden loss of power. She might be on some kind of strong chemical therapy; there seemed to be a correlation between the aura she exhibited and the auras of some cancer patients I had recently seen. Fairly typical in such cases, or when some type of radiation is used on a person, the aura shows large gaps or is very weak and depleted, in need of major replenishment.

The treatment of cancer, with its debilitating side effects, can be almost as devastating as the disease. When viewing the aura, it can be impossible to distinguish between the disease and the effects of the treatment, but I believe that, whatever the cause, I saw in Virginia's aura the telltale effects of cancer.

Another woman I had worked with about that time had an inoperable tumor in her chest. She had received massive amounts of chemo and radiation therapy, and the tumor pressing against her bronchial tube and aorta had reduced to the size of a baseball. When I first visited her, she looked quite healthy outwardly and told me nothing of what was wrong with her, wanting me to discover, if I could, what her problem was. As I placed my hands around her auric field, I was surprised to find a very clearly defined area in her upper torso that literally shot out random sparks that felt like the lit end of a sparkler had been placed in my palm, only more pronounced. This was so strong a sensation that I knew at once radiation had been recently employed, masking any feeling of the tumor itself.

So it was with Virginia Kelly. Although I was unable to accurately feel her aura because of the circumstances, the visible effects in the aura were quite clear, even though outwardly she looked to be in the peak of health and on top of the world.

This close encounter with the mother of the president proved to be an interesting counterpoint to my experience with the parents of the vice president, Al and Pauline Gore. I had been with them at a dinner party just a few months before my plane ride with Bill Clinton's mom, and the difference in demeanor and aura was striking.

Al Gore Sr. had himself been a well-known politician for several terms in the Senate and in many ways gave the impression he was the one still running for office. Here, he was in the situation of trying to restrain his normal flamboyance so as not to upstage his more conservative son.

Mrs. Pauline Gore was the ever-dutiful wife and proud mother, presenting herself with a calm reserve, leaving the limelight for her husband and son. She was frequently referred to in her husband's speech and used as an example of common sense and practicality in an uncommon and sometimes impractical political world. The calm eye of the swirling whirlwind, she was also reputed to be quite a comedienne, all of which seemed to make Pauline wince and squirm ever so slightly, even as she sat smiling and staring up at Al Sr. on the dais as he spoke.

When they were seated together and talking quietly, their auras could be seen to be melding together and equalizing, which frequently happens with couples married for many years. (You can see this effect yourself when practicing the exercises mentioned earlier with two people standing face-to-face.) Even with individuals who are total strangers, this coalescing effect can happen fairly rapidly, but try it with married couples, and the phenomenon should be more pronounced.

With Albert Gore Sr., what was interesting was watching the evolution from his "at rest" aura to the various changes that transpired throughout his speech. The effect of an audience on the performer's aura can be readily seen in most cases, and as he spoke, all the usual traits began to manifest themselves, such as increased glow and size, with a color change from orange to yellow happening only after he was more than halfway into the speech.

As the former senator became more relaxed after telling some jokes about himself and the family, he started picking up steam and auric vibrancy as he spoke of his onetime political differences with his son concerning Vietnam. As the old stump speechmaker started heading for home with exhortations to vote for his son, a warm golden glow enveloped and energized both him and his wife Pauline.

After dinner, they were quite gracious and animated, never meeting a stranger, it seemed, and spending several minutes with everyone who wanted to talk with them. Now they were inhabiting the same golden yellow bubble, even while conversing separately with different individuals. If not starting to physically resemble each other, as some married couples do, their auras at least were well in tune with one another, exhibiting a sum greater than (and different from) their individual parts.

"I just can't get over having Albert on what is going to be the winning ticket in this election. We've got to get the Democrats back in the White House, and I know he'll be a positive influence, so you've got to get out there and support him, support the whole ticket, bring Alabama in as a state that voted Democratic. . . ." Even off the podium, Al Sr.'s blood was up, and the fire was still burning. Hopes were rising, and the polls looked good, if only they could carry this momentum through to victory.

There was the strangely tentative sense of victory in the air, almost as if everyone was afraid to really believe it, lest defeat be snatched from the jaws of apparent victory. After all, Jimmy Carter and Walter Mondale were the last Democratic ticket voted into the White House, and that was sixteen long years ago. . . .

Twelve years before, I had witnessed this scene in reverse. Just after the Carter/Mondale defeat in 1980, I was invited to Walter and Joan Mondale's house for dinner by the girl I was dating, the daughter of a Democratic representative from Maine. Melissa and I, along with her sister and date, were at the Mondale's with Bronson Clark, the girls' father.

We talked about everything but politics before dinner, focusing on Joan's extensive collection of modern and postmodern American art. She really loved these works by Motherwell, Rothko, and de Kooning, and she glowed with a close to the body but bright and fuzzy pink aura as she took us on a tour of the house. This was the most animated and happy she appeared all night, her aura increasing in size and radiance as she spoke about each piece of art.

None of us really shared her level of enthusiasm, but Joan was in her own world and seemed liberated there in her private home, away from a public life that could not have been much fun for her at that time. As a patron of the arts, she could find solace in promoting something she truly loved, putting away any need to present a politically correct persona. The pink color she exhibited showed a pure heart and an air of innocence, at least while she was surrounded by the art that provided a refuge from the political reality of the moment.

As dinner progressed, she seemed to recede in vibrancy, and after dinner—as the talk gradually began to touch on politics—Joan seemed abstract and withdrawn, adding very little if anything to the discussions. A forced air of conviviality predominated the remainder of the evening, conversations taking on a leaden inevitability with the focus subtly shifting toward finding out about who this boyfriend of Melissa's was.

The combination of election loss and the resultant underlying mood made for a challenging experience that evening, poles apart from the feeling of impending victory I was to experience with the soon-to-be vice presidential family more than a decade later.

Politics varies from entertainment in several fundamental ways (although they've been compared more directly since the election of our first actor-president): If a performer has an off night, there's always tomorrow. When a politician loses, it can be years, if ever, before vindication occurs.

It is no wonder, then, that the auras of politicians tend to be very different from those of entertainers. When giving a speech, a politician is performing and subject to the audience-actor dynamic, but that is where the similarity ends. Politicians I've seen up close, whether winners or losers, show a darker, deeper shade of whatever color they radiate (frequently navy blue) and seem very controlled and compact in radiance, extending no more than one or two inches. Perhaps this shows the mental control politicians consciously exert to maintain a politically correct persona.

13

Auras in Love

*What we think, what we
visualize, and what we feel
all play a major role in the
image our aura projects.*

In my class on auras, one of the most popular segments demonstrates the effect of interpersonal proximity on the aura. You might have heard about so-called chemical attraction—or repulsion—individuals experience when they first come in contact with each other. While this certainly happens (through the secretion of pheromones), there is another less-documented exchange also taking place: the bioenergy transfer. This exchange can now be seen as well as felt. We know the changes that occur when you change the pattern of your breathing. We have seen the changes that occur when crystals are brought within proximity of your body, and in fact—depending on the crystal—the effect is not always a positive one. What we think, what we visualize, and what we feel also play a major role in the image our aura projects.

Imagine, then, the impact that another individual has on your energy field. To see this effect, you merely need to stand two people face-to-face, approximately one foot apart, against a wall, stand back eight feet, and look at them. Be aware that the auric shapes around the profile of the bodies are slightly different from those when viewing the aura from directly forward. There is an area in front of the nose and mouth extending out to the throat area that moves out, in a ball shape, away from the face. When viewing the aura, be aware that there is a natural tendency for an egg shape to occur from the top of the head around the front and back of the body. It does not follow the shape of the nose, mouth, chin, and throat as it does when you view the aura from directly ahead.

When you see people standing face-to-face at a one-foot proximity for the first time, it is common to be able to see their individual auras first and then—very quickly—to see whether their auras are coming together or pulling apart. It is not uncommon when a man and woman who are strangers first stand face-to-face for one or the other of their etheric fields to pulse to the forward or backward position in opposition to the forward or backward pulse of the other person. Frequently we will see in class where a man's aura may actually start to creep forward when facing a woman, and the woman's aura may actually deplete in the front and be visible as a very bright line coming out her back; that is, the aura of the man seems to be invading her space, and her aura is trying to get away from it as fast as it can! There are some cases where just the reverse will be true: the man's aura will actually be duller in the front and brighter in the back as the woman's aura moves into his space. After a few minutes, however, this will typically settle down, and you may actually begin to see lines begin to appear between the foreheads, from eye to eye, in the throat area, or from heart to heart.

It is not uncommon to see a ball of energy—which typically is a dark mass—hovering between the throat and upper chest areas of two people standing face to face for the first time. Married couples, however, will typically show a more uniform auric presentation, and in fact will frequently have very similar colors and radiant fields, depending upon their ultimate comfort around each other and compatibility. Between people who are very comfortable being around each other, it is sometimes possible to view the auras as one.

Two Auras as One

It is not beyond the realm of possibility to see this field yourself in the mirror when you are with someone that you care about. Use the exact same technique that you have learned in earlier chapters, and you will be able to note where each energy field stops and starts and whether there is a good vibe between you. Although it is preferable to stand face-to-face for this energy transfer to occur, it is still possible (and much easier to see in the mirror) when standing side by side.

Seeing the energy field around the two bodies simultaneously is more difficult than seeing individual auras, especially when you are first learning to use this technique. Again, don't focus on the foreground—continue to look past the outline of the two bodies, whether looking in the mirror at your own or viewing another couple's aura. It is always imperative to continue to focus past the images. Don't get caught up looking at facial expressions or so-called body-chemistry postures. Be aware that discrete bands of light may be visible between the foreheads, throat areas, or the heart areas, and note that these fields are very clearly defined. Obviously, since these linkages are visible, there must be some energy transfer occurring in these areas.

Be patient when first learning this technique, because it is more difficult to see than individuals' auras. In the classroom environment, we have tremendous fun—sometimes almost holding mini singles events—with the various energy fields present among the participants readily on view!

I have had the opportunity to go on extended cruises where I have been a presenter on auric technique and where we've had the good fortune of having couples from newlyweds to fiftieth-anniversary celebrants on board. This variety has allowed all of the participants to see the great differentiation between the auras of these couples. One couple celebrating their golden anniversary stayed after class to have their auras read. Many of the people who were standing around after class were amazed to actually see a unified field around the two of them. This unity was also striking in that their individual auras were so similar as far as color, shape, and intensity were concerned. It was quite obvious that they had a very unified energy field and presentation.

More embarrassing, however, are the couples who may be struggling. This will also be readily apparent to first-time viewers. Keep in mind that while this should not be used in any invasive way, this auric vision does give us an added insight and an ability to look at couples in a new light. Whether you use this informally with yourself and your loved one or as a tool to determine ultimate compatibility, it should be used only with the permission of all participants.

You can also see the effect love has on an individual's aura. When viewing your own aura in the mirror, think of someone that you love, and then try to feel that emotion of love that you are sending and receiving from that person. Your aura will get stronger and brighter immediately. Likewise, when viewing someone aurically, ask them to think of someone that they love, and you will see an immediate change registering in their field, as well. That is why it is so exciting to see two people face-to-face who are in love, because the bands of energy will be quite clearly defined and very visible, especially in the heart area and in the third-eye area. Ask the two people to look into each other's eyes. Frequently it will become instantly apparent that there is a visible channel of energy that acts as a bridge between them, most usually visible in the line between the eyes.

I am frequently asked to look at couples to determine whether their energies are compatible, and it is amazing how readily apparent that compatibility is based on viewing the aura. With a little practice, you will be able to determine in yourself and in others how open your heart chakra truly is, and how much of an introvert or extrovert you are in matters of the heart.

14

Auras near Death

Having glimpsed the Big Picture, many near-death experiencers find emotions such as fear, impatience, and hostility usually cease to be of concern. One of the greatest benefits, however, is the elimination of fear, particularly the fear of death.

One of the most talked-about phenomena in the last quarter century is the near-death experience (NDE), during which someone dies, or appears to be close to death, yet returns to this life with stories about a "world beyond." An estimated thirteen million people in this country alone have had this startling experience. Many books, movies, magazine articles, and TV shows have examined NDEs or other out-of-body (OBE) experiences that do not involve actual clinical death, but are similar in nature. The real number of experiences is likely even greater, since many people are reluctant to talk about something so extraordinary and unbelievable that "normal" people might think them crazy.

Reports of these experiences tend to follow many, if not all, of these common threads:

A sense that the person has left his or her body and is floating directly above it.

An omniscient view of the area, with a detailed understanding of what is being done by others present, especially common during emergency medical procedures or surgery.

Passing through a tunnel or dark space toward a bright light.

Finally arriving at the loving light, which is indescribably radiant and warm, attractive, and supremely peaceful.

Full knowledge and understanding of everything. You become part of the universe and know your place in it.

Seeing others, some of whom you might recognize as deceased family members or friends.

Watching a vivid movie of your life pass before your eyes, highlighting both the positive and negative aspects contained therein.

A realization that this is not yet your time to go, or the feeling of coming to the end of your (cosmic) rope, at which point you suddenly return to your body.

The actual duration of the experience in temporal time might be only a few seconds, or it could last an hour or more in rare cases. But to the experiencer, there is no correlation to time as we know it. In fact, there is very little correlation to anything we think we know in our normal reality.

Words cannot describe these out-of-body experiences any better than we can describe color to a blind person or music to a deaf-mute. Imagine what it would be like to have lived in a cave your whole life then suddenly find yourself outside in the warm sunlight—surrounded by oceans and mountains, farmlands and forests, experiencing all of this simultaneously for the first time in a kaleidoscopic panoply—and then having to go back to your cave and explain it all to the others, who know life only as it exists inside that cave.

Even this analogy does not fully describe the overwhelming sensory and emotional overload caused by these experiences. Common initial responses given by most OBE and NDE individuals, when asked to relate what happened during their "trip," are:

"Words can't describe it at all."

"Language is inadequate to convey the feelings."

"You've got to experience it, then you'll know."

"It's like nothing in this world."

"I can't put it in words, but I didn't want to leave!"

NDEs and OBEs often cause life-altering behavioral changes in those who have the experience. Perhaps OBEs are even responsible for many mystical and religious conversions, such as Paul's epiphany on the road to Damascus when he encountered "the light" and became a follower of Christ instead of a persecutor of Christians. In fact, the Bible is full of mystical experiences that could be attributed to some type of OBE. Mystics of all religious faiths speak of transcending earthly bounds, glimpsing heaven briefly, then returning to speak of the wonders they have seen. Universal truth, beauty, wisdom, and, above all, the unlimited power of love resonate through these experiencers, who might use their cultural traditions or religious beliefs to describe and personify this loving light as a manifestation of God.

Most people who have these experiences do not set out to save the world, but they do gain a different perspective on life. Some actually withdraw from previous career paths or change directions toward service for others rather than continuing to chase financial or material accumulation.

Many near-death experiencers report profound changes in their attitude toward people in general, and family and friends in particular. Having glimpsed the Big Picture, many near-death experiencers feel emotions such as fear, impatience, and hostility usually cease to be of concern, and these sometimes radical changes can be mystifying for those around them.

One of the greatest benefits of the near-death and out-of-body experience is the elimination of fear, particularly the fear of death. Everyone whom I have spoken to, read about, or seen on TV who has had these experiences tells of liberation from the fear of dying.

We might not lose the fear of pain and suffering or the sense of grief and loss when someone close to us dies, but the actual transition out of this life no longer causes any fear or dread. For many experiencers, the idea of death can almost be described in terms of "going home."

While there is no longer a fear of dying, there also seems to be no increase in wanting to die among experiencers. There are more than 100 people included in an ongoing study by Dr. Bruce Grayson at the University of Connecticut, which tracked the lives of suicide-attempt near-death experiencers over a time period of as long as twenty years. Research done on the case histories of NDE among suicide attempts shows a zero incidence of repeat attempts. That is, those who had the near-death experience while attempting to commit suicide have all subsequently chosen to live, while non-NDE suicides continue at the normal repeated attempt rate of 80 percent. Whatever happens to people who have these experiences (which science is still at a loss to explain), the data certainly indicate profound changes in behavior and lifestyle.

Rather than choosing to die, near-death and out-of-body experiencers become more attuned to life. Each day becomes more intense, relationships more intimate, time more precious. Many NDEs report the love and needs of their children or some unfinished business with family members as the primary factor in their return to this existence. There is a reason why we are here (although the specifics may still be hidden from us after a near-death experience), and it is this sense of mission that intensifies lives after a NDE or OBE and prevents people from "checking out" of this life prematurely.

In my own case, these experiences have had a profound impact, perhaps due to their early and frequent occurrence; I've always felt "directed" and very blessed. Even as a small child, I had an awareness and acceptance of a world beyond. This strong link with spirituality was reinforced by a 1950s-era Catholic-school education. Yet I was rebellious and considered "different" by my grade-school peers. My parents might say "difficult," but curiosity about almost everything I encountered led me into the trouble in which I frequently found myself. After realizing at age eleven that I had an unlimited potential (and strong attraction) to commit mischief, I also knew that I was on Earth to utilize my talents for positive purposes, and I pledged to do so one spring night as I lay in bed thinking and praying just before my twelfth birthday.

Each successive out-of-body experience made me more aware of my calling, which has now led me through several career changes and various geographic locations. Having been fortunate enough to successfully experience life from many perspectives, I've never felt limited or lonely, just lucky and loved.

Even though I have never married or found my soul mate, I have had some wonderfully deep and passionate relationships. Every friend or lover has taught me something, but I guess I'm still supposed to continue learning. I do want to have a child and hope one day to have this paramount life experience, but perhaps the NDE and OBEs I have had are the only (re)birth experiences I will ever know. If so, my life has been—and continues to be—extraordinarily full and happy.

Were the NDE and OBEs the primary cause of this happiness? I don't think so, but they did offer a particular insight that certainly helped me overcome setbacks and enabled me to place failures and disappointments into a larger perspective.

Did these out-of-body experiences change my ability to see auras? Again, I don't think so, because anybody can see the aura, not just near-death and out-of-body experiencers.

Will the aura change after this type of experience? It probably does, but I've never done a before-and-after study. I can say that the auras of people I've met individually or at near-death and out-of-body symposia who have had these experiences seem to be a little brighter and more radiant than those of the average people I might see on the street or in one of my classes. There is something about a person who has had this type of experience that might not be readily apparent at first, but as the conversation turns to subjects relating to certain topics (spirituality, life after death, philosophy, states of consciousness, et cetera), an almost agitated level of enthusiasm can frequently be noticed. This excitement is what causes the higher energy display seen in the aura and is a major factor in an NDE or OBE aura, although in general it can be noted that any high emotions increase auric flow and visibility.

And yet there is an uncommon sparkle that these people show in their auric fields that is in some ways similar to that previously described as belonging to charismatic people. The difference seems to be in the frequency of the vibration, with the charismatic person exhibiting a slower, lower, more physically exciting vibration, while the near-death or out-of-body experiencer's vibration is faster, clearer, and more ethereal.

Although there doesn't seem to be a particular color associated with either NDE, OBE, or charismatic persons, the colors they do possess are quite bright and radiant. The quality of the energy projected in the aura seems more focused or clear, and frequently there seems to be much more quantity, as well.

Clairvoyance and Auras

Some aura readers and psychics don't actually see colors when they view the auric field; they base their often startling insights only on the energy level they see and feel. Recently my aura was read by one such person, who didn't know that I was writing a book on the subject. In fact, she knew nothing about me at all.

Ginny Stringer sat me down in her naturally lit office in front of a white curtain. Referred to her by one of my students, I was fascinated to see just what someone else's technique for viewing auras would be. Judging from her setup and professional environment (no incense, hanging beads, or gypsy costumes), we were off to a good start.

Ginny told me that she only interpreted the energy a person projected and did not see colors in the aura at all. She proceeded to tell me several details of my recent past that were too specific (and accurate) to be coincidental. "I see you've been in a dentist's chair recently but haven't been there in a long time. You're also going back again next week."

That was true. Two days prior, I'd had a molar temporarily crowned on my first visit to a dentist in almost three years—and I was returning for the permanent crown in less than a week.

"Do you have sinus problems?"

I said, "No."

"I'm getting a sinus drainage, and I don't have any allergies or a cold myself, so if you don't have the problems, someone close to you does." I thought a minute and remembered that my girlfriend was a chronic sinus and upper-bronchial inflammation sufferer, but before I could say anything, Ginny said, "You are in close personal or work-related contact with two women who have this problem." My secretary had left work early just the previous day with a severe case of sinusitis.

Before I could respond, she continued, "One of the women is about to make a big change. I see her taking off a badge with her picture on it and moving far away." She pantomimed the action of unclipping the badge and held it out as if she would give it to me. I realized this was true, as my secretary was in her last month of work, about to move to another state, and that I, as the staff human-resources person, would take her badge as she departed the company.

Clearly, something special was happening here, and Ginny was on a roll. But how could she be seeing this from my aura? I certainly couldn't foretell the future or describe the recent past by looking at an aura.

Or so I thought.

After she told me I would meet my wife (how did she know I wasn't already married?) in about eighteen months at a lecture I was to give concerning a paper I had written, her husband walked into the office and handed her a message. He looked at me briefly and then left. I was struck by how white and fuzzy his aura looked, and I could feel the physical and emotional pain radiantly pour off him in waves.

When my reading was over and I told her that I, too, could see auras, she wanted immediately to know what I saw in her husband's aura. "Tell me about his health . . . how long do you think he has yet to live?" Startled by her questions, I protested that I had only seen him for a few seconds, not long enough to form any in-depth opinions, and that it certainly wasn't a habit of mine to tell people if they were about to die. "Go on, you know very well he's ill. If you can see auras, you should be able to see his pain—its location, its intensity—and if you see that, then you'll know about the rest. . . ."

As I recalled his brief entrance into the room, I saw again the white and gray aura and remembered how fuzzy he looked. Although I've never experienced it, there are various accounts of persons not boarding airplanes or elevators at the last second because they felt death was imminent or saw in the faces of the people gathered before them something terminal. It was this same type of intuition that I felt when I thought about the man and his faint, pale aura.

Pain seemed to be radiating from him consistently, and his expression could be described as a tightly controlled grimace, his posture slightly stooped, and his gait more a shuffle than a walk. To guess his age would be difficult, but he was probably younger than he looked—yet this could be readily ascertained by looking at him with my regular vision. His auric characteristics were in keeping with the overall physical condition and had many of the elements of one who is about to transit from this life.

My new auric friend pressed me for more details. "When is he going to die? Weeks, months, years . . . What do you see?" Flippantly, I responded, "It almost looks as if he wants to die, and very soon too, based on his white aura." White is the color of either very saintly persons or ones about to depart this life.

"Excellent! You really do have the vision. He wanted to commit suicide last night, and I've hidden his gun again today. He's been talking about wanting to die for a while now, and I'm afraid he just might do it. I've got to watch him all the time. . . ."

Once again, my skepticism was confounded by the events. Trusting my instincts instead of logic allowed me to stumble into a correct assessment of a situation I would not have believed was within my power, even after I had just witnessed the same type of clairvoyant assessment done on me. This introduction to the clairvoyant nature of aura reading is something that I continue to explore.

Conclusion

Reflecting on Our Auras

*Within our grasp, we have the ability
to control our health and well-being
on a day-to-day basis. Learning about
the aura is one way to gauge and monitor
our health on an entirely different scale.*

I have been accused of being hardheaded, but after all this time and all these discoveries, you would think I'd be completely amenable to the mysteries of life and to the possibility that we are capable of so much more than we know.

Well, I'm not totally there yet.

Unfortunately, there are many of us who are totally shut off from exploring anything new or different, especially something as different as exploring our capacity to see and feel the human aura.

That's a shame, because these extraordinary capabilities—however we come by them or in whatever form they take—allow us to glimpse our transcendent spirituality and are a foundation for our link with the Divine. Ironic, then, to think that the use and mastery of these talents—whether aura reading, energy healing, astral projection, clairvoyance, or handwriting analysis—are natural expressions of our human nature, as well.

Most of us are searching for truth and meaning in life. As we approach the millennium, many are becoming more concerned with deeper questions and probing past the superficial issues, interested more in root causes. The age-old questions of "Who am I, and what am I doing here?" are still with us (and mostly unanswered) but are augmented by more global concerns such as "How are we going to coexist on this tiny planet without destroying ourselves and our fragile environment?" There is a growing sense that time is running out and that we must change old habits and perceptions in order to survive. Of course, this is not true for all of us—there are the professional naysayers.

These cynics and backward thinkers have existed in every culture, and the world today is plagued by their actions. Unfortunately, some of them are in positions of power around the world. Real enlightenment rarely comes down from the top; instead, social, political, and spiritual repression are the norm rather than the exception throughout many parts of the world. Individuals progress much faster than social structures as a whole, and there must be an enormous number of frustrated individuals who are many steps ahead of their respective governments in their desire to grow and prosper. Tragically, several pockets of savagery around the world don't look like they will submit to change any time soon.

With nationalism and even tribalism on the rise since the end of the cold war, these retro "antiglobal" forces are the major stumbling block facing humanity on its inevitable path toward true global unification. China, Russia, and Japan have operated as insular societies for so long that it may be generations before nationalistic bastions such as these truly integrate with the rest of the world on all levels. Nonsecular countries such as Iran will take even longer.

Nevertheless, the inhabitants of these nonsecular countries historically have been among the most advanced and enlightened in art, literature and philosophy. The governments of these countries, however, have been among the most repressive.

Are free thought and spiritual enlightenment an escape from social oppression? Or are repressive governments a conservative reaction to "dangerous" anarchist liberal thought? Dangerous to whom? Governments and social institutions of all types are in business to stay in business, but they might be out of business if the freethinkers of the world ever got together.

We've seen pictures taken by the astronauts that show the Great Wall of China as the only man-made line of demarcation visible anywhere on the planet. Other than that, no evidence of individual countries exists on Earth when viewed from space. Yet we have a natural inclination on Earth to think always in terms of "us" and "them."

So imagine for a moment that UFOs really exist. I'm not saying that they do exist (remember I'm still a little skeptical), since unlike auras, I've never seen one, but suppose they landed on the White House lawn and in capitals around the world in broad daylight.

What would be the immediate effects of such an event?

With this uncontrovertible evidence that we are not alone in the universe, do you suppose we might start to think and act more globally? When the idea sunk in that there was something different out there, and that the universe comprised other sentient species than just us, would we start to behave in a more communal fashion? Politics as usual would start to look awfully petty and cease to exist in short order. Nationality would become trivial and would be replaced with specialty. Concerns about Serbia versus Croatia would be replaced by concerns about Earth versus Alpha Centauri. Global thinking would become the norm, not the exception. We would soon become the United States of Earth.

Maybe the citizens of planet Earth already know this intuitively. The vast majority of us believe in other life-forms in the universe, even if we are skeptical of the reports of alien abductions and flying saucers with little silver-suited men who come from a different dimension. This belief in some form of nonhuman life might explain our increasing cynicism about politics as usual, as well as our disgust at the self-serving, short-sighted interests of many of our politicians and world leaders.

The religions of the world, as well, would all lose their grip as the various denominational differences evaporated in the face of alien epiphany. Since all religions are man-made attempts to put God in a bottle—or rather, in their temple—and since God has always been viewed by each religion as humankind's creator and personal savior cast in our own image and likeness—news of competing species more evolved or advanced than our own would obliterate humanity's (and religions') exclusive relationship with the Divine.

Yet it is this divine relationship in each one of us that shines through on a personal level and transcends ethnosocial and politico-religious differences. Once again, we are for the most part aware, at least on the subconscious level, that something much greater than us exists and that we are somehow absolutely intertwined with it. This might explain why fewer of us go to church, but more of us consider spirituality very important in our lives.

We possess an insatiable hunger to discover our supernatural nature and have an unquenchable thirst for knowledge about our link to the everlasting. The truly enlightened ones among us are busy at work, ready to unlock any door to this knowledge that can be found, with science and the arts both converging on this same target. Perhaps at no time in human history have more people sought this knowledge across so many various fields of endeavor. Humankind is knocking on the cosmic portal with a battering ram.

True, some say, "Don't go through that door," afraid to disrupt the status quo. Some even refuse to admit the existence of the door, let alone what might be behind it. But the genie is out of the bottle, and humanity has tasted the fruit from the tree of knowledge. There is no turning back, even if it helps once in a while to look back in order to remember and build on the knowledge already gained (and lost) over the eons. In our rush to find the answers to our questions of today, it would be foolish to forget the lessons of the past. After all, hubris, or arrogance, was the one unforgivable sin in ancient Greece. To be guilty of it allowed no room for divergent opinion by others and placed the smug perpetrator at the self-proclaimed pinnacle of wisdom (and in peril of his or her life).

"Blessed are those with eyes to see and ears to hear," but "more blessed still to believe and not to have seen." Some things do come down to faith, and much about life is still (thankfully) a mystery. It wouldn't be much fun if we knew everything, now, would it? But if we do know something is real, something we have experienced yet cannot explain or prove scientifically, the skeptics still need to recognize that mysterious things can still be real.

Living as we do in this modern age, which could be called a technocracy, one part of us wants to believe only in "proven reality." But reality might be many possibly contradictory levels of existence. If you believe that we possess a soul, then we are spirits trapped in the material world. If you believe that there are dimensions of existence beyond this space-time continuum, then is this the "real" reality, or are we trapped in an illusionary construct? Science is starting to bump into questions about life that sound suspiciously like they belong in the realm of the philosophers and theologians, who in turn are finding surprising solace in scientific discovery, thus narrowing what used to be an unbridgeable chasm between these competing worlds of thought. While we do exist in this time and space we call reality, occasional tantalizing glimpses beyond the boundaries happen every day. Dreams, intuition, precognition, prayer, meditation—even various art forms—transcend this existence and point toward a different reality. Sadly, so does the epidemic use of mind-altering drugs (and an alarming suicide rate), especially among teenagers. There seems to be a natural longing to leave this existence, if only for a while, through movies, books, music, or travel, all of which temporarily engage our imagination and transport us to an alternate reality on a daily basis.

Now you can use another way to consciously explore this human duality of incarnate spirit. It is demonstrably real in this reality and brings us to an alternate awareness of ourselves and others. Everyone has it.

Anyone can see it. Science can measure it, even photograph it. Mystics have talked about it for centuries. Artists have depicted it, healers have used it, and we have all felt it: the aura is a very special physical manifestation of our human duality.

Can we change the world with this knowledge of how to see the aura?

No, at least not immediately.

Will it bring a better understanding of who we are and what we are all about?

You bet it will!

As individuals, we also have within our grasp the ability to control our health and well-being on a day-to-day basis. Learning about the aura is one way to gauge and monitor our health on an entirely different scale, and this knowledge can be used to augment our growing awareness of the effects that various aspects of our environment have on us. With luck, we might also be able to say that in the next five or ten years, 80 percent of our total knowledge of self will have been gained. The capability is there; we must learn about and then use this knowledge. Don't let fear or the naysayers hold you back.

Our conditioning against the belief in otherworldly or extrasensory events is very strong. Auras are just one more thing we have been conditioned to believe could not possibly exist. That certainly was my first reaction when I was taught to see them. But as I became comfortable and adept at seeing the aura, I began to realize how natural and "this-worldly" our visible magnetic and electric field had become. Piece by piece, my resistance and skepticism have been crumbling.

As you become more adept at seeing the energy field around yourself and others, you might become curious, as I did, about related fields of study. If you already have interests in these areas, auric perception will hopefully augment your knowledge. Too often we look for answers everywhere but where real knowledge resides, which is within the self. Auric vision, once attained, is but one threshold crossed in a journey to further self-knowledge and fulfillment.

Appendix I

Auric Exercises

The following two exercises instruct you how to see the aura both on yourself and on others in ten simple steps. The diagrams show proper viewing position and the two layers of auric fields that surround us.

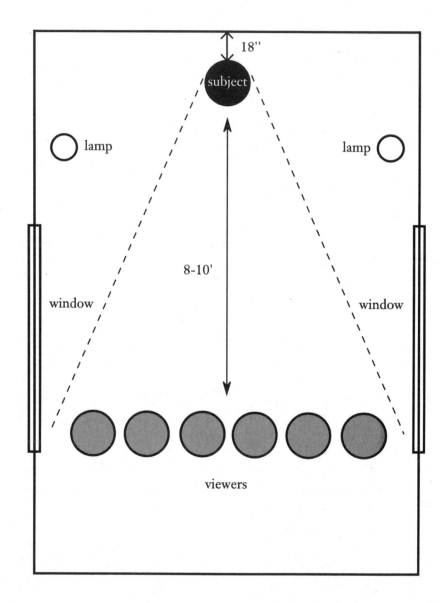

Illustration 1: Viewing Diagram

To See an Aura

1. Stand the subject eighteen inches to two feet in front of a bare white wall. Avoid walls with colors or patterns.

2. Use indirect lighting—natural ambient daylight, if possible. Avoid fluorescent light or direct sunlight.

3. View the subject from at least ten feet away.

4. Ask the subject to relax, breathe deeply, and rock gently from side to side with hands unclasped at his or her side.

5. Look past the subject's head and shoulders and focus on the wall behind him or her.

6. Avoid looking at the subject, concentrating instead on the texture of the paint or whatever surface is behind him or her.

7. As you look past the outline of the body, where the air starts and the body stops you will see a band of fuzzy light around the subject, about one-quarter inch to one-half inch in depth. This is the etheric aura.

8. Continue to look past the outline of the body, and you should see the subject as if he or she is illuminated from behind, sometimes with a bright yellow or silver color. One side might glow more brightly or slowly pulsate. Auras rarely are uniform.

9. Each person is different. Some subjects will have less-visible auras than others, and every viewer will not always at first see colors. The fuzzy envelope or halo around the body will be discernible within a very short time—usually one minute or less.

10. Try using different subjects and experiment with lighting and background. Soon you will see a second, larger band of light three inches to two feet around the body. This is the astral aura. It is usually darker and more diffuse.

To See Your Own Aura

1. Stand in front of a mirror at least eighteen inches away, farther if possible.

2. Place yourself with a white or neutral color surface visible in the mirror behind you.

3. Relax, breathe deeply, and sway gently from side to side.

4. Focus on the texture of the surface of the wall behind you.

5. As you stare past the outline of your head and shoulders, you will see the envelope of light around your body move with you as you rock gently.

6. Remember to breathe as you do this, since you are now both viewer and subject.

7. Lighting should be subdued, neither too bright nor too dark. Experiment. Auras cannot be seen in total darkness, and bright light will wash out all but the most vibrant of auras.

8. Color of clothing is unimportant. You might find that your auric color, when you become accustomed to seeing it, will clash with certain items in your wardrobe, but you will see your true colors regardless of what you wear.

9. Experiment with projecting a color. Think of a color and try to visualize it. You can change your base line color temporarily through this kind of exercise, and the change can be seen.

10. As you exhale, the aura should get larger. Reciting the numbers one through thirty in a normal speaking voice will help liberate your energy. Take a breath after every two numbers. Speed up the count from the number twenty on without taking a breath and watch your aura change in size and vibrancy. As you resume normal quiet breathing, the aura will return to its former size but might appear a little brighter.

Guide to Illustration

Everyone can see the first etheric auric layer, which is closest to the body, and is usually the brightest. The second astral auric layer is farther away from the skin, and more diffuse. Be aware that the colors will change and blend together in these two fields, seldom having a distinct line of separation between them.

The following diagram on page 128 is included, then, as an approximate location guide only. No two auras are alike, and even the same person's auric presentation frequently changes. The tremendous variety of auric fields you will see as you practice viewing them is limited only by the number of subjects viewed.

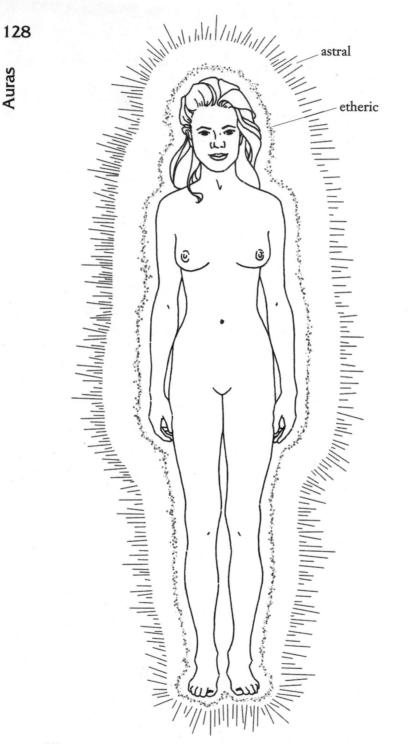

astral

etheric

Illustration 2: Etheric and Astral Auras

Appendix II

Color Meanings and Locations

Colors have certain emotional characteristics that have been recognized in most of the world's cultures for centuries. This guide may be used as a basis for analyzing this relationship and the general areas of the body affected by these colors.

Color Chart

purple	Spiritual attainment, divine connection, mystical understanding, cosmic consciousness. "Purple raiment." Located in the pituitary gland.
indigo	Inspired thought or deep wisdom. Can show spirituality and devotional nature. Artistic and harmonious with nature. Self-mastery. Located in the pineal gland.
blue	Strong mental powers, intelligence, logical thinking. Clear blue shows intuitive capabilities; "out of the blue." Dark shades show over-analytic, suspicious nature or visionary mentality. Centered in the brain.
green	Balance, harmony, healing, the calming force. Clear green shows adaptability, versatility. Dark shades are deceitful, jealous; "green with envy." Located in the thyroid and neck area.
yellow	Love and kindness, compassion, optimism; "Breath of life." Dark, lifeless yellow shows suspicion, covetousness. Centered in the solar plexus and heart region.
orange	Energy and health, physical vitality, dynamic force. Pride can result from an excess of orange in the aura. Dark or cloudy orange shows low intellect. Centered in the stomach and spleen area.
red	Physical life, vitality, ambition, sexual power. Dark or cloudy red shows violent or passionate tendencies; "red with rage." Centered on the genital area.

Other Colors

scarlet	Lust, lower passions, materialism.
rose pink	Selfless love, gentleness, modesty.
brown	Avarice, selfishness.
gold	Higher self, good qualities, harmony.
silver	Versatility, high energy, constant change.
gray	Depression, low energy, fear.
black	Sinister, malice, evil intent.

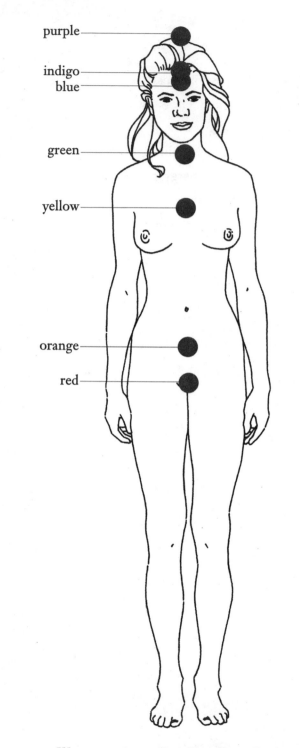

purple

indigo
blue

green

yellow

orange

red

Illustration 3: Chakra Colors

Colors Relating to Chakras of the Body

purple   chakra 7
             Spirit

indigo   chakra 6
             Third Eye

blue   chakra 5
             Mind

green   chakra 4
             Thymus

yellow   chakra 3
             Heart

orange   chakra 2
             Spleen

red   chakra 1
             Genital

Suggested Readings

Andrews, Ted. *How to See and Read the Aura*. St. Paul, Minn.: Llewellyn, 1991.

Dale, Cyndi. *New Chakra Healing*. St. Paul, Minn.: Llewellyn, 1996.

Jackson, Carole. *Color Me Beautiful*. Reston, Va.: Acropolis Books, 1980.

Karagulla, Shaficia. *Breakthrough to Creativity*. Los Angeles, Calif.: DeVorss, 1967.

Tansley, David. *The Raiment of Light*. Rutledge & Kegan Paul: Melbourne, Australia: 1984.

Index

138

How to See and Read the Aura

Ted Andrews

Everyone has an aura—the three-dimensional, shape-and-color-changing energy field that surrounds all matter. And anyone can learn to see and experience the aura more effectively. There is nothing magical about the process. It simply involves a little understanding, time, practice, and perseverance.

Do some people make you feel drained? Do you find some rooms more comfortable and enjoyable to be in? Have you ever been able to sense the presence of other people before you actually heard or saw them? If so, you have experienced another person's aura. In this practical, easy-to-read manual, you receive a variety of exercises to practice alone and with partners to build your skills in aura reading and interpretation. Also, you will learn to balance your aura each day to keep it vibrant and strong so that others cannot drain your vital force.

Learning to see the aura not only breaks down old barriers, it also increases sensitivity. As we develop the ability to see and feel the more subtle aspects of life, our intuition unfolds and increases, and the childlike joy and wonder of life returns.

0-87542-013-3
160 pp., mass market, illus.   **$3.95**

Aura Reading for Beginners

Richard Webster

When you lose your temper, don't be surprised if a dirty red haze suddenly appears around you. If you do something magnanimous, your aura will expand. Now you can learn to see the energy that emanates off yourself and other people through the proven methods taught by Richard Webster in his psychic training classes.

Learn to feel the aura, see the colors in it, and interpret what those colors mean. Explore the chakra system, and how to restore balance to chakras that are over- or under-stimulated. Then you can begin to imprint your desires into your aura to attract what you want in your life.

These proven methods for seeing the aura will help you:

- Interpret the meanings of colors in the aura
- Find a career that is best suited for you
- Relate better to the people you meet and deal with
- Enjoy excellent health
- Discover areas of your life that you need to work on
- Imprint what you want in your future into your aura

1-56718-798-6
208 pp., 5 3/16 x 8, illus.   **$9.95**

To order, call 1-800-THE MOON
Prices subject to change without notice

New Chakra Healing

Cyndi Dale

Break through the barriers that keep you from your true purpose with *New Chakra Healing*. This manual presents never before published information that makes a quantum leap in the current knowledge of the human energy centers and fields and the principles that govern the connection between the physical and spiritual realms.

By working with your full energy body, you can heal all resistance to living a successful life. The traditional seven-chakra system was just the beginning of our understanding of the holistic human. Now Cyndi Dale's research uncovers a total of 32 energy centers: 12 physically oriented chakras and 20 energy points that exist in the spiritual plane. She also discusses auras, rays, kundalini, mana energy, karma, dharma, and cords (energetic connections between people that serve as relationship contracts). In addition, she extends chakra work to include the back of the body as well as the front, with detailed explanations on how these energy systems tie into the spine. Each chapter takes the reader on a journey through the various systems, incorporating personal experiences, practical exercises, and guided meditations.

1-56718-200-3
304 pp., 7 x 10, illus., softcover   **$19.95**

To order, call 1-800-THE MOON
Prices subject to change without notice

Chakra
Therapy

Keith Sherwood

Understand yourself, know how
your body and mind function, and
learn how to overcome negative programming so that you
can become a free, healthy, self-fulfilled human being.

This book fills in the missing pieces of the human anatomy
system left out by orthodox psychological models. It serves
as a superb workbook. Within its pages are exercises and
techniques designed to increase your level of energy, to
transmute unhealthy frequencies of energy into healthy
ones, and to bring you back into balance and harmony with
your self, your loved ones, and the multidimensional world
you live in. Finally, it will help bring you back into union
with the universal field of energy and consciousness.

Chakra Therapy will teach you how to heal yourself by healing your energy system because it is actually energy in its
myriad forms that determines a person's physical health,
emotional health, mental health, and level of consciousness.

0-87542-721-9
256 pp., 5¼ x 8, illus., softcover   **$9.95**

Wheels of Life

Anodea Judith

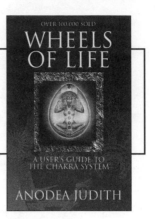

An instruction manual for owning and operating the inner gears that run the machinery of our lives. This second edition, written in a practical, down-to-earth style, will take the reader on a journey through aspects of consciousness, from the bodily instincts of survival to the processing of deep thoughts.

Discover this ancient metaphysical system under the new light of popular Western metaphors: quantum physics, elemental magick, Kabbalah, physical exercises, poetic meditations, and visionary art. Learn how to open these centers in yourself and see how the chakras shed light on the present world crises we face today. And learn what you can do about it!

This book will be a vital resource for all those who are concerned with holistic growth techniques.

The modern picture of the chakras was introduced to the West largely in the context of Hatha and Kundalini Yoga, and through the Theosophical writings of Leadbeater and Besant. But the chakra system is equally innate to Western Magick: all psychic development, spiritual growth, and practical attainment is fully dependent upon the opening of the chakras!

0-87542-320-5
544 pp., 6 x 9, illus., softcover   **$17.95**

Aura Energy for Health, Healing & Balance

Joe H. Slate, Ph.D.

Imagine an advanced energy system that contains the chronicle of your life—past, present, and future. By referring to it, you could discover exciting new dimensions to your existence. You could uncover important resources for new insights, growth, and power.

You possess such a system right now. It is your personal aura. In his latest book, Dr. Joe H. Slate illustrates how each one of us has the power to see the aura, interpret it, and fine-tune it to promote mental, physical, and spiritual well-being. College students have used his techniques to raise their grade-point averages, gain admission to graduate programs, and eventually get the jobs they want. Now you can use his aura empowerment program to initiate an exciting new spiral of growth in all areas of your life.

1-56718-637-8
288 pp., 6 x 9 $12.95

Book Order Form

❏ **How to See and Read the Aura** Andrews   3.95
     Order #L013-3
❏ **Aura Reading for Beginners** Webster   9.95
     Order #K798-6
❏ **New Chakra Healing** Dale   19.95
     Order #K200-3
❏ **Chakra Therapy** Sherwood   9.95
     Order #L721-9
❏ **A Chakra & Kundalini Workbook** Mumford   16.95
     Order #K473-1
❏ **Kundalini and the Chakras** Paulson   14.95
     Order #L592-5
❏ **Wheels of Life** Judith   17.95
     Order #L320-5
❏ **Aura Energy for Health, Healing & Balance** Slate   12.95
     Order #K637-8

U.S., Mexico & Canada	
Orders $15 and under	$4.00
Orders over $15	$5.00
International Airmail	
(Add the retail price of each book)	
UPS Second Day Air (U.S. Only)	
One book	$8.00
Each additional book	$1.00

Subtotal _____

Shipping _____

Total Enclosed _____

Charge Card:
❏ MasterCard   ❏ VISA
❏ American Express

Card No. _____

Exp. Date __ __ /__ __   M.C. Bank No. __ __ __ __

Signature _____

Name _____

Daytime Telephone (____) _____ ext. _____

Mailing Address _____

City, State, Zip _____

Complete and mail this form to:
Llewellyn Publications
P.O. Box 64383, Dept K643-2
St. Paul, MN 55164-0383
or call toll free:
1-800-THE MOON